Term

WINDOWS OF LIGHT

Windows of Light

*Using Quartz Crystals as Tools
for Self-Transformation*

Dr. Randall N. Baer
and Vicki Vittitow Baer

1817

Harper & Row, Publishers, San Francisco

*Cambridge, Hagerstown, New York, Philadelphia
London, Mexico City, São Paulo, Singapore, Sydney*

FIRST EDITION

Library of Congress Cataloging in Publication Data

Baer, Randall N.
    WINDOWS OF LIGHT

    Bibliography: p.
    1. Occult sciences.   2. Quartz crystals—Miscellanea.
I. Baer, Vicki Vittitow.   II. Title.
BF1999.B24   1984   133   84-47823
ISBN 0-06-060325-9

84 85 86 87 88 10 9 8 7 6 5 4 3 2 1

Dedicated to the Merkabah

CONTENTS

FOREWORD

I have always been drawn to crystals. As a small child my parents were disconcerted when they bought me a toy, a Handy Andy tool kit, and I promptly emptied out all the tools, ignoring them completely, and instead enjoyed myself immensely by filling the empty toolbox with rock crystals I collected from beaches, streambeds, and rock shops. At the time I did not think much of my preference for crystals over toys. Even as I grew older, the implications of my attraction to crystals remained elusive to me, but my love of crystals remained.

It was well into my adult years that I received a letter from a talented psychic. Hidden amongst his comments (the vast majority of them startlingly accurate) was the assertion that in a former incarnation I had been very involved in using crystals as magnifiers of psychic power. One of the methods I employed in this incarnation—which he alleged to have been an Atlantean one—was to house quartz crystals in pyramids to charge them with energy. As I sat at my desk reading the letter in which he conveyed the information, my gaze traveled over to a beautifully crafted wooden pyramid sitting before my typewriter. Inside it was a large amethyst crystal I had placed there. What was disconcerting to me was that the action had been entirely unconscious on my part. The pyramid had been a gift and I had placed the crystal in it quite unthinkingly. I was aware of the notion of pyramid power at the time, but I had certainly not given any conscious thought to charging the crystal by placing it in the pyramid. The box had merely seemed a handy receptacle. It was then that I started to wonder more about my unconscious attraction to crystals.

As I started to research the matter further, I quickly discovered that there was a lengthy and widespread history to the notion that crystals can magnify psychic energy and healing powers. People as distant from one another as the Australian aborigine and the Yuman-speaking people of southern California and adjacent Baja California consider the quartz crystal a "living" or "live rock." My friend, anthropologist Michael Harner, tells me that crystals are one of the objects that shamans universally regard as power objects. Both the Yualai and the distant Tsimshian of the Northwest Coast of North America "sent" the quartz crystal or its spirit to fetch the image of a particular person. A shaman of the Jivaro of the Amazon keeps a crystal in his monkey-skin shoulder bag along with all his other power objects, as does the present-day Paipai shaman. The Mexican Huichols believe that the souls of shamans return to the Earth in the form of quartz crystals and the Warao shamans of South America put quartz crystals in their medicine rattles because they believe that such crystals are "spirit helpers" and will assist in extracting harmful intrusions from the bodies of their patients.

Why are crystals so universally regarded as power objects? It can be argued that crystals are aesthetically appealing and therefore are more likely to catch the eye of a shaman, but butterfly wings are equally aesthetically appealing. Why are there not widespread traditions of butterfly wings being used for healing purposes? Even more remarkable, ancient traditions are very specific about the types of crystal that may be used as power objects, and quartz figures prominently. Some have suggested that this is because quartz is transparent, a rare quality for an object to have in nontechnological societies. However, in *The Way of the Shaman* Harner points out that mica is also transparent, but he knows of no similar traditions in shamanic literature about mica.

I stumbled across what I think may be a clue to the lengthy traditions about crystals while researching quite a different matter. In my book *Mysticism and the New Psychics* I asserted that a creature's DNA doesn't seem to explain everything about how the creature develops and evolves. For example, at a certain stage of embryonic development, the cells of an organism can be mixed up, but they will then *unshuffle* themselves and once again where they belong. Somehow heart cells know they are heart cells and cornea cells know they belong in the cornea. This is unusual, for each cell contains exactly the same genetic blueprint, the same DNA. How, then, does a heart cell know where to reposition itself? If each cell contains nothing but an identical copy of the same blueprint, where then is the builder that tells them where they belong in the design? To explain this mystery, I advanced the notion that there existed organizing fields, as yet unrecognized by any science, that govern the form and structure of living organisms.

Shortly after my book came out in 1981, a Cambridge biologist named Rupert Sheldrake published a book entitled *A New Science of Life* that proposed exactly the same notion. As Sheldrake sees it, not only are the form, development, and behavior of living organisms shaped and maintained by these as yet unknown fields, which Sheldrake calls morphogenetic fields, but the fields themselves are molded by the behavior of *past* organisms of the same species through direct connections across both *space* and *time*. To support his version of the notion, Sheldrake cites such evidence as the fact that rats of a particular species are able to perform better on a test in England after rats of the same species (but different genetic lines) have learned to perform the same test in the United States.[1]

What really caught my eye in Sheldrake's book was his assertion that living organisms aren't the only things that have morphogenetic fields. According to Sheldrake, the form and development of crystals also seems to be governed by morphogenetic fields. For example, in *Crystals and Crystal Growing* A. Holden and P. Sanger relate an incident that happened to a chemical company in the early 1950s. The company was involved in growing large single crystals of ethylene diamine tartrate for industrial use. About a year after the company first got involved in the practice, some workers noticed that the crystals in one of their growing tanks had begun to grow badly. A new and previously unknown crystal had started to develop, an *anhydrous* form of ethylene diamine tartrate instead of a *monohydrate* form. Unfortunately, no matter how often the workers disposed of the new crystal, it quickly reappeared and spread, soon supplanting the old form. It even started to appear spontaneously in other factories. As Holden and Sanger state, "During three years of research and development, and another year of manufacture, no seed of the monohydrate had formed. After that they seemed to be everywhere.''[2]

Holden and Sanger point out that this strange sort of survival of the fittest often takes placed when chemists develop new substances that do not occur naturally on the Earth. When the substance is crystallized for the first time, it seems uncertain as to which crystalline form it will assume. Varying forms seem to vie with one another until a victor is found. Then, from that time on, all other crystals of the substance will follow the blueprint laid out by the winning form. As Sheldrake interprets it, this is because crystals, like living organisms, are governed by morphogenetic fields. In other words, it is the winning morphogenetic field that establishes the blueprint that all other subsequent crystals of a substance follow, and that is why the same crystalline structure will begin to appear spontaneously in different factories widely separated by space and time.

What intrigues me is the notion that living organisms and crystals have something so in common. One is once again eerily reminded of the Yuman shaman's reference to the quartz crystal as a living rock. After encountering Sheldrake's work, I started to wonder more and more, if what Sheldrake was saying was correct, why should crystals of all things possess a quality that was inherently biological?

Of course, much of this is only speculation, but I did come across a possible answer to this question, a partial answer to be sure, but one that has a certain poetic resonance to it. One of the long-standing puzzles of molecular biology is how did life originate on the Earth in the first place? We now know that the environmental conditions of the early Earth would have been very advantageous for simple organic substances to grow. If one duplicates the atmosphere and waters of the primordial Earth in a laboratory and runs an electric current—a bolt of lightning—through it, one can quite easily create simple organic molecules, ribose and glucose sugars, and even nucleoside phosphates—the precursors of DNA. Nonetheless, these are still a far cry from the total complexity of substances necessary for the creation of life. Take, for example, insulin. It has been calculated that even if the whole Earth were composed of amino acids and if this massive volume of amino acids rearranged themselves randomly and completely ten times a second for the entire duration of the Earth's history, there would still have been little chance of producing, even for one-tenth of a second, one molecule of insulin.

Alexander Cairns-Smith, a biochemist in Glasgow, points out another problem. If such a primordial soup of amino acids did exist on the early Earth, the development of life may even have been seriously hampered by it. For example, Cairns-Smith observes that such a primordial soup would have been an extremely reactive chemical environment. Thus, any sugar that happened to develop in the broth would quickly have reacted with the surrounding chemicals and turned into a sticky caramel. Cairns-Smith asserts that life as we know it probably could not have evolved from such a corrosive soup. In fact, he believes that life originated, not as the result of a biochemical mechanism but as the result of a different mechanism entirely.

As for what that mechanism was, Cairns-Smith first asks: What is one of the central qualities that defines life? The answer to this is, most obviously, the ability to reproduce or self-replicate. Self-replication provides continuity and enables evolution to occur. Without it, life could not exist as we know it today. To the question of what was the original self-replicator, the most primitive gene, current biological thought alleges that it must have been the DNA molecule itself. However, Cairns-Smith again finds this highly doubtful. As he points out, DNA is an extremely fragile molecule on its own. It is easily broken by physical stress and would have been quite ripped apart by the ultraviolet light in the sunlight raining down on the Earth.

But if the first self-replicators were not DNA molecules, what were they? To answer this question, Cairns-Smith begins by listing the other qualities that the most primitive genes had to possess. In addition to being able to self-replicate, they had to self-organize under simple conditions. They had to be able to acquire and retain information and then use that information to interact with their environment. And they had to be able to reproduce copies of themselves that also contained the information. Is there something, even simpler than DNA, that possesses all these abilities? Yes, says Cairns-Smith, that something is crystals.

Crystals are dramatic examples of the capacity of matter to self-organize. As we saw in the incident related by Holden and Sanger, they can also acquire and retain information—for example, their geometric structure—and reproduce copies of themselves containing the same information. Given that they perform all these functions while remaining far more stable and durable than DNA, Cairns-Smith believes that crystals make very likely candidates as the most ancient progenitors of life. However, to more fully establish his case, Cairns-Smith knew that he had to find a crystal that possessed one further quality, the ability to use the information it possesses to interact with its environment.

Ice crystals, for example, respond to their environment but don't really interact with it in anything approaching a complex way. Similarly, salt crystals tend to just sit there. However, Cairns-Smith did come upon one crystalline form that not only interacts with its environment in a complex and ordered way but actually seems to possess an innate tendency to evolve. That crystalline form is a colloidal suspension of quartz particles in water, more commonly known as clay.

Clays not only have the ability to grow and absorb other molecules, but they can then incorporate the information from those molecules and use it to alter and change themselves. Clays were also most certainly among the most abundant substances on the early Earth. Even while the Earth was still too hot to support life as we know it, cooling rains poured down upon the mountains and the rocks, slowly pulverizing them into vast percolating beds of clay. Cairns-Smith believes that it was clay itself that formed the first link between life and nonlife. In his book *The Life Puzzle* he sketches out a possible evolutionary description of three different species of clay he calls Sloppy, Sticky, and Lumpy.

In Cairns-Smith's view, Sloppy was most probably the first species of clay. Living in slow-running streams and gathering "food" in the form of clay-forming sediments, Sloppy was an open-structured type of clay that could quickly trap lots of food and thus spread rapidly over the streambed and shore. Sloppy's only downfall, due to its loose, open structure, was that the first rainfall would quickly wash Sloppy away. Thus, Sloppy was always on the endangered clay list. Sticky was a more selective type of clay. Instead of only gathering clay-forming sediments, Sticky also absorbed some of the sticky caramels resulting from the corrosion of sugarlike organic molecules that occurred naturally in the primordial broth. Thus, Sticky was able to fasten more firmly onto rocks and keep from being washed away during storms. However, Sticky's sticky sugar molecules also tended to make it sedentary and inhibit its travels, and thus its influence.

Lumpy solved this problem by accidentally picking up just enough organic molecules to make it both a little sloppy and a little sticky. Having the thick, coagulated consistency of modern clays, Lumpy was able to grow rapidly, survive storms, and even spread, sending broken lumps of itself downstream to grow into new claybeds. In this way Lumpy not only interacted in a complex manner with its environment but also survived selective pressures. Add just one more trait to Lumpy—the ability of crystals to apparently duplicate and pass on innovation—as demonstrated by Holden and Sanger's crystals of ethylene diamine tartrate—and you have everything necessary for the acquisition and inheritance of new characteristics, a quality hitherto believed confined to the realm of biological life.

Cairns-Smith believes that clays were the first "movers" on the face of the Earth. He also believes that clays and naturally occurring organic substances formed an early marriage and that it was as a result of this marriage that organic materials ultimately acquired the ability to reproduce and pass on inherited characteristics from their crystal forefathers. If this sounds farfetched, Cairns-Smith points out that Armin Weiss, an American chemist, has shown that some clays, particularly the mica types, can build up extensive patterns of organic substances between their silicate plates. Weiss has identified more than eight thousand different derivatives in which clays have acted as templates, causing chemicals like ammonium ions and alcohols to solidify into organic components. Cairns-Smith points out that such reactions could easily give rise to polymers with what can only be called genetically controlled configurations. In the early Earth, as more and more of the formation in such silicate templates was transformed into organic molecules, Cairns-Smith believes that it was inevitable that the clay would ultimately have assumed a secondary role, providing little more than a protective clamp, until at last, life broke free and started to form its own protective cell walls.

Of course, Cairns-Smith's ideas are at present only theoretical, but in reading them, one cannot help but recall that he is not the first to assert that life on the Earth was brought forth from the clay. Equally stirring is the curious coincidence that the major component of clay is a granular form of that silicate we have come to know as quartz. Is our species' universal attraction to that mysterious crystal due to the fact that in some intuitive way we understand that it is quite literally our most ancient ancestor? I do not know, but I cannot help but wonder if the power and draw of crystals is due to the fact that perhaps we are more closely related to them in kind and energy than our scientific understanding has previously suspected.

Michael Talbot
New York City
February 1984

Just as the rainbow appears in the Heavens as a sign of God's Love and Light to mankind, so does the crystal come forth from the Earth to bring a message of Light from the past as a promise of Love for the future.

—Sananda

PREFACE

Quartz crystals are the manifestation of the Creator's finest hour of expression. They are windows of light with many facets which show the myriad dimensions of life created from cosmic dust in an ever expanding universe. Divine plan has foreordained that all expanding life revolve around one common denominator, quartz crystal. Through frozen solidified light all creation could be monitored and assisted through the evolutionary process.

From ancient times to the present day, quartz crystals have been a source of Light to mankind. Highly valued by spiritual leaders and healers as well as scientists, the unique attributes of quartz have played a key role in mankind's evolutionary development. For quartz is the crystal connection to the infinite octaves of Light; it is a spiral staircase to crystalline perfection. Just as water freezes into ice and yet can be transformed into the higher-energy state of steam, so too can pure White Light "freeze" into quartz crystal, yet retain the potential to be activated into a window for the higher-energy states of Light to shine through to the earth-plane. Quartz is unique in this regard and as such serves as a looking glass of the soul, reflecting back to us the Light-beings that we truly are.

The current time period in Earth's history marks a turning point of great proportions as a new era of consciousness transformation unfolds. As this process has gained momentum, increased awareness of the unique importance of quartz crystals has been activated. Indeed, it is a subject that has gained a considerable degree of focused attention within only a few years' time. This growing awareness reflects the expansion of collective consciousness as we regain areas of key knowledge that will aid in manifesting a new world order, known by many as the New Age. As the realms of physics, metaphysics, and holistic health unify more and more, a Divine Meta-Science will emerge, bearing Light-based technologies that will catalyze an individual and collective transformational process of a grand order. Crystals are focal components within this spiritual science and as such are "keys" to doors willed with potentials beyond present dreams.

It is our sincere desire that this book will serve as a catalytic function in the process of disseminating information, rediscovering ancient knowledge, and stimulating further systematic investigation concerning the multifaceted dimensions of crystal-Light. Our deepest hope is that these tools will be used wisely, as the Light that they are. Truly, they are messengers of the celestial realms. Let us go forth as one towards ever-expanding spirals of Light-transformation.

Chapter 1

HISTORICAL PERSPECTIVES

Windows of Light into the Past

The use of quartz throughout human history is a recurring Light-motif. From the highly advanced ancient civilizations to the primal medicine man to the present day, crystals have been used on many levels for a multitude of purposes. As we survey the many-faceted applications of these windows of Light throughout history, it becomes clear that they serve as both guide and pathway toward upward spirals of evolutionary transformation. Through this process of synthesis and remembrance, we gain further recollection of our ancient heritage and greater insight into our present-day regenesis.

Within primal cultures the world over, the figure of the shaman, or medicine man, is recognized as a focal point of spiritual attunement and authority. Classically, shamans are defined as "technicians of the sacred,"[1] ones who enter ecstatic trance states and venture into the Otherworlds of Spirit. In these realms, shamans enact rituals of discovery, propitiation, cure, and salvation; they retrieve lost souls, guide the souls of those who have died, and directly communicate with the cosmic powers-that-be. These ancient mystic-healers serve to defend life, health, and fertility—the world of "Light"—against death, disease, and disaster—the world of "darkness."

They are in communication with the world of gods and spirits. Their bodies can be left behind while they fly to unearthly realms. They are poets and singers. They are not only spiritual leaders but also judges and politicians, the repositories of the knowledge of the culture's history, both sacred and secular. They are familiar with cosmic as well as physical geography; the ways of plants, animals, and the elements are known to them. They are psychologists, entertainers, and food finders. Above all, however, shamans are technicians of the sacred and masters of ecstasy.[2]

As an intermediary between the realms of Earth and the Heavens, the shaman is a guide, a channel, a vision, an image, and a personification of Light.

Significantly, quartz crystals are integrally associated with the entire shamanic complex. From ceremonial rattles and costume artifacts to initiatory rites and healing tools, crystals pervade shamanism as it has occurred in diverse cultures throughout the centuries. In Australia, Siberia, North America, South America, and Africa, the use of quartz appears as a recurring theme. These ''stones of Light'' function as a rainbow bridge across the thresholds of the Earth into the celestial realms. It is only fitting that these shamanic warrior-priests should use the Light of crystals with which to perform their crucial roles of mediumship, protection, and healing.

The archetypal cosmology of shamanism portrays crystals as solidified Light originating in the supernal realms. Although fallen or brought down to Earth, crystals give the shaman both a bridge to the heavens and a key to supernormal powers associated with celestial beings. In Australia a celestial figure named Baiame throws them down from the heavens.[3] Moreover, most shamanic candidates around the world receive crystals as part of their initiatory rite of passage. Many such initiates find themselves in a ''place of Light'' with rock crystals glittering from the walls. They are given several of these and told how to use them.[4] In the Malay Peninsula the shaman uses crystals obtained from ''spirits of the air, water that is magically solidified, or fragments that the Supreme Being lets fall from the sky.''[5]

The shamanic initiatory process is one of dying to the earthly body of flesh and being reborn to the adamantine crystal-body, or Light-body. During this process, crystals are abraded, swallowed, or inserted into the initiate's body.

. . . [H]e throws the candidate into the sky, ''killing him.'' Once they are in the sky, the master inserts small rainbow serpents . . . and quartz crystals (which have the same name as the mythical Rainbow Serpent).[6]

. . . [T]he candidate must silently submit to an operation performed by two old medicine men. They rub his body with rock crystal to the point of abrading the skin, press rock crystals into his scalp, pierce a hole under a fingernail of his right hand, and make an incision in his tongue.[7]

Some initiates have a piece of quartz "sung" into their foreheads.[8] Another method involves pouring "liquefied quartz" over the candidate's body.[9] The archetypal theme here is one of remaking the "dead" body of the initiate by incorporating the solidified Light of quartz into a new crystalline Light-body. The new shaman is then able to enter the many celestial Otherworlds and to perform his many sacred duties with impunity.

Crystals are shamanic power objects par excellence. Shamans ascribe a singular importance to quartz above all other power objects, perceiving it to be a "live rock," a living being. As such, crystals are regarded as the most powerful of the shaman's "spirit helpers." To know the keys to activate and employ this solidified form of living Light is to become a man of power and the ways in which this power is used are manifold. Many of these supernormal abilities are associated with seeing, that is, amplified inner sight. Many shamans are able to "see right into things[10] in the manner of x-ray vision. In fact, quartz is the only power object that appears the same whether the shaman is in a normal waking state of consciousness or in an ecstatic trance state.[11] Thus the crystal functions as a window that activates access to multidimensional octaves of Light and the resultant extrasensory and supernormal talents. Indeed, shamans are able to perceive past, present, and future events through powers of divination. They are also able to perceive disease conditions and the means to correct them.

. . . [C]enoi [spirit helpers] are believed to live in these magical stones and to be at the shaman's orders. The healer is said to see the sickness in the crystals; that is, the cenoi inside show him the cause of the sickness and the treatment for it. But in these crystals the hala [shaman] can also see a tiger approaching.[12]

Northwest Coast shamans send crystal spirit helpers to fetch the image of a particular person. When the image has arrived, rattles with crystals inside are used to extract a harmful intrusion or disease condition from the image.[13] In medicine bags, crystals are used as a center of power, emanating their Light- and Life-giving properties throughout the other diverse power objects, acting to energize them and to maintain their full potency. In ecstatic trance states, crystals are used as a catalyst and a rainbow bridge to project the soul to the Otherworlds. Once there, the shaman experiences these heavenly realms with full conscious awareness and is able to interact with various beings that are encountered. These and other applications of the crystal power object demonstrate the multidimensional Light inherent in quartz. It is certainly no mistake that shamans around the world would collectively recognize the dynamic potentials of this "live rock."

The shaman's crystal is the primal forerunner of a diversity of subsequent applications. As many of the shaman-based hunting-and-gathering cultures transformed into agricultural societies, the spiritual and metaphysical fabric of mankind's culture changed greatly. With increasing degrees of organization and complexity, the unified role of the shaman as collective artist, healer, priest, mystic, and psychic protector divided into such specialized roles as alchemists, psychics, magicians, doctors, mystics, and priests. As this occurred, the ways that crystals were used diversified considerably according to intentionality, specialized knowledge, and depth of spiritual understanding. In general, this whole time period reflects an instinctive attraction to the Light of quartz, though often knowledge was somewhat clouded by folklore, myth, and lack of in-depth insight. Save for a few adepts, mankind manifested but a hazy reflection of the highest applications. Nevertheless, the "sparks" of insight that do shine through demonstrate the ongoing conscious and subconscious recognition of the Light-properties of crystals.

Echoing the shaman's recognition of quartz as solidified Light, the root word of quartz crystal originated in the Greek word *krystallos*, "ice." For many centuries it was believed that crystals were actually ice frozen so hard that it could not melt. One common ancient legend held that crystals were originally holy water that God poured out of heaven. As it drifted toward Earth, it became frozen into ice in outer space. This holy ice was then petrified by various angels so that it would forever stay in solid form for the protection and blessing of mankind.[14]

Throughout these centuries, quartz has been used in many ways, prized for its mystical, mythical properties. One of the earliest pieces of evidence for this is found on an inscription on a Babylonian cylinder seal of about 2000 B.C. It reads: "A seal of Du-Shi-A [quartz crystal] will extend the possessions of a man and its name is auspicious.''[15] In ancient Tibet the eastern region of heaven was thought to be made of white crystals. In Japan quartz has been a symbol of the purity of the infinity of space and also of patience and perseverance. Crystal gazing, also known as crystallomancy, has been used by many seers, psychics, and political leaders for aeons. Divination of the past, present, and future has played a key role in the decisions of many of the most powerful leaders in history. The amethyst (purple quartz), too, was a highly prized and influential stone, valued for its abilities to endow the wearer with quickening of intelligence and invulnerability in battle. Its special virtue was the capacity to cure or prevent drunkenness, in the sense of being drunk with the illusions and passions of the world. Its purple coloration symbolizes royalty and was esteemed for its properties of aiding spiritual growth and its ability to impart spiritual power. A rare stone in earlier centuries, it is found in the crowns, rings, staffs, and jewelry of royalty and the higher levels of religious hierarchies. In the Catholic church, it is the stone of the priest and the bishop and is also found on the Pope's Fisherman's ring. The crozier of a Catholic bishop, his pectoral cross, the altar stones, the candlesticks, and certain crosses carry seven main stones, quartzes among them. These seven stones are diamond or clear quartz, sapphire, jasper, emerald, topaz, ruby, and amethyst. In the Episcopal cross the amethyst is placed in the middle with the sapphire under it, the diamond above it, and amethysts placed at the extremities. In the altar of the Free Catholic Church, six gemstones are placed around a central quartz crystal. It is often the case that either diamond or clear quartz was used in the central place of religious settings. This was done due to their transparency and clarity, which attracts pure White Light and helps to reinforce and centralize the more specific color emanations from the surrounding gemstones. The radiations from these groups of precious stones were thought to attract a complete spectrum of spiritual energies and to help activate them within man's inner being.

On another level, there have been a relatively small number of alchemists, ''wizards,'' and magicians through the centuries who have known and applied various ''secrets'' of the alchemical science of crystal energies. Through combining various gemstones and metals in conjunction with crystals in highly specific and complex ways, "power wands" were created that would serve as powerful amplifiers, modulators, and projectors of focused thought-forms and cosmic energies. Essentially, these wands were highly tuned, very responsive scientific devices attuned to the individual-specific thought frequencies of the operator. In this way, these devices became an extension of the self, acting like a radio receiver, tuner, and transmitter of focused thought-energy. Fairy wands and wizards' staffs are mythical reflections of this reality. Similarly, the bejeweled crowns and staffs of kings and queens were no accident, being made by the more skilled craftsmen-alchemists as powerful energy generators.

The more precious stones one wears, the more strongly will they be charged with cosmic forces, which they will radiate out into their surroundings. That is why a monarch used to wear so many jewels, in order to turn himself into a living battery of power for the nation.[16]

The high priest breastplate is another manifestation of this basic principle. This breastplate was composed of twelve different precious stones arranged on a silver plate in three vertical rows of four stones. These stones were sard, agate, chrysolite, garnet, amethyst, jasper, onyx, beryl, emerald, topaz, sapphire, and diamond; of these, amethyst, jasper, onyx, and agate are of the quartz family. The specific placement of these minerals created a complex coding pattern of vibrations that the high priest could selectively use to attune his consciousness to a single vibration or specific combinations of frequency patterns that would aid in the performance of the various priestly functions. Thus, we see the power wands of alchemists, the crowns and staffs of monarchs, and the high priest breastplate as higher harmonic applications of crystal science, echoing the advanced crystal technologies of the ancient civilizations and pointing toward the recollection of such knowledge today and tomorrow.

Throughout the Earth's history many superadvanced civilizations have inhabited this planet. These were societies of beings with advanced spiritual development and high degrees of scientific knowledge. In addition to the relatively well-known cultures of the Atlanteans, Egyptians, Mayans, and Lemurians, there have been the Cyclopeans (Els), Oraxians, Poseidans, anti-Atlanteans, Uramorans, and numerous others. In many of these civilizations the quartz crystal was a key, powerful technological tool that played a wide variety of significant roles. For many centuries knowledge concerning these peoples and how they used crystal science has been veiled. As a new era of global evolution unfolds, the time is ripe for a greater degree of remembrance of this information through many sources.

The seeding of the Earth-plane from the stars and the celestial realms has taken place at numerous times in this planet's history. These "seeds of Light" were groups of souls who agreed to specific missions to uplift the less highly evolved souls within the Earth's karmic energy field on both spiritual and technological levels. These civilizations were intended within the patterns of the Divine plan to facilitate a collective quantum leap of consciousness for this jewel of the Heavens known as Earth. Many times the door was open for the fulfillment of the Earth's destiny as a Light-house literally in the Heavens, an emerald within the fourth-dimensional frequencies of Light. However, time and time again these peoples failed in the highest aspects of their mission due to a giving in to the lower frequencies of the Earth field. The desire for personal power, born of spiritual ego, created a number of situations in which their highly advanced technologies were used in spiritual ignorance as means of control of others and self-aggrandizement. The crystal-based technologies were perverted by a relatively few, very powerful individuals. The time comes now again in this the twentieth century to lift the Earth into higher octaves of Light, there to start anew as a shining crystal in the Father's Kingdom. Let us learn the lessons of history well.

Atlantis is the most famous and well known of these ancient civilizations. The Atlantean culture was one of disciplined lifestyle and intellectual-scientific focus. In addition to the field of crystal science, the realms of sonics, computers, particle-beam and laser technologies, pyramidology, and radionics were also very advanced. Crystals, though, were the central technological building block around which all the other aspects revolved. In essence, crystals were used as the primary means to generate a wide spectrum of energies that could be modified and distributed throughout the entire civilization. Perfectly symmetrical and faceted crystals as large as 25 feet in height and 10 feet in diameter were used as the primary energy generators. Legends and channelings from various sources speak of the Tuaoi stone as one of the many ''firestones'' that acted as these energy generators.

As for a description of the manner of construction of the stone: we find it was a large cylindrical glass . . . cut with facets in such manner that the capstone on top of it made for centralizing the power or force that concentrated between the end of the cylinder and the capstone itself. . . . The building above the stone was oval; or a dome wherein there could be . . . a portion for rolling back, so that the activity of the stars—the concentration of energies that emanate from the bodies that are on fire themselves, along with elements that are found and not found in the earth's atmosphere.[17]

A continent-wide system of similar crystals created a network of energy that was used for basic energy requirements of the entire society.

. . . [S]torage of the motivative forces from the great crystals that so condensed the lights, the forms of their activities, as to guide the ships in the sea and in the air and in conveniences of the body as television and recording voice.[18]

Other examples of ways in which this energy was used include antigravity devices, photographing at a distance, electrical devices of many kinds, crystal lasers, the creation of force fields, interdimensional communication, and more.

The Atlanteans also had a very sophisticated series of thirteen healing temples that used crystals as part of the Light-based healing technologies. The Great Healing Temple, for example, was used to assist in accelerating an individual's rate of evolution and for specific healing functions. In the central healing hall was a table made of an alloy containing silver, ground crystal dust, and copper. The pedestal that supported this table was shaped like a pyramid and made of quartz. The ceiling was domed and composed of interlocking crystals of various colors in patterns of ancient symbols. ''When the light shone through the roof it was a brilliant, yet soft, strong pastel. It was soothing and yet awesome, for it was an exquisite pattern of color and vibrations.''[19] Many of the healing methods involved energizing the crystals with a laserlike beam of precise energy frequencies. Specifically faceted crystals were also used for different forms of psychic surgery, disease diagnosis, tissue and limb regeneration, and the healing of all forms of disease.

In another healing temple, called the Temple of Dolphins, was a room with ceiling, floor, and walls composed entirely of crystal. This chamber was used for initiations and for interdimensional travel and communication. One example of its use is as follows:

When it was necessary for an individual in that civilization to receive training and teaching spiritually, he would enter the room, sit in a chair. Depending upon the frequency of vibrations he was attempting to reach, different size crystals on a form of pulleys were brought into focus. . . . If the source of the communication to be received was of a higher frequency than the receiver was able to accommodate, the crystal acted as a step-down, or relay station. It lowered the frequency of the vibrations to make them compatible with the one receiving the information.[20]

Also in this temple crystal lasers were used to accelerate an individual's evolutionary growth process by focusing pinpoint insertions of specific frequencies of energy into the mind, which created an increase in the vibrations of the soul. In this way, the knowledge and growth of many centuries could be facilitated in various individuals at appropriate times.[21]

The crystal technologies of the Atlanteans, then, were highly sophisticated and very powerful indeed. Through the centuries of their development, though, a certain few highly placed individuals started to misuse these energies for their own selfish purposes. The use of cybernetic mind control of the masses through projected beams of energy, brain implants, drugs, and hypnosis came to pass. Some of the most powerful crystals, the ''terrible, mighty crystals,'' were modified into weapons of war. These ''Sons of Belial,'' as they were called, made war against the ''Sons of the Law of One'' and also performed dangerous experiments with genetic engineering and the ''firestones,'' thus creating a series of mighty conflicts and upheavals of the earth that culminated in the destruction of most of the people and the sinking of the entire continent. While it is well to learn the historical lesson that crystals are extremely potent tools that can be used either with Light or in spiritual ignorance, it is also appropriate to realize that the greater part of the Atlantean culture performed many important services in its own time and has passed on numerous contributions to future civilizations.

Another civilization called Orax existed in the area of Siberia approximately 150,000 years ago. At that time, this area was a lush, temperate zone. The entire culture existed under a magnetic dome of energy created through a crystal-based force field. Around the perimeter were placed several thousand crystals that served as grounding points for the magnetic dome. The power to these crystals was generated from a central core of crystals and conducted to the perimeter crystals through a system of copper rods. Energy could be tapped from many areas along the copper rod grid system to furnish energy for various technological functions. These rods, six feet below the surface, also served to make the ground very fertile for growing crops, creating a veritable paradise. When entry into the magnetic dome was desired by a visiting ship, the power to specific crystals was turned off, thereby creating an opening for entry.[22]

The Incan, Mayan, and Egyptian civilizations possessed a sophisticated knowledge of crystal technology in conjunction with pyramidology. Many of the creators of this advanced scientific knowledge were reincarnated Atlanteans or highly evolved souls from other galactic star systems sent on specific missions of service to Earth. Most of the numerous pyramids of these cultures were created by master builders and craftsmen using the lost arts of sonic levitation, crystal laser quarrying, and thought-form technologies. Originally some of these pyramids were covered with white marble, a micro-crystalline form of quartz, carved with precise sequences of universal signs and symbols. These carvings were part of the total energy pattern of the pyramid that, when combined with the pyramidal shape, served to produce a diversified energy field capable of performing many functions. Among those functions were 1. to control and balance the Earth's electromagnetic energies and to unify them with the total energy pattern of this solar system and other star systems; 2. to receive, modify, amplify, and project massive amounts of energy for many purposes, including healing, initiation, interdimensional communication and monitoring, electricity generation and distribution, and others, utilizing crystals at key locations within the pyramids; 3. to fuse space, time, and matter to create a vortex, or interdimensional doorway, through which beings from other worlds and dimensions could conveniently pass and be in a protected environment while traveling to and from Earth; 4. to provide a beacon for interplanetary travelers; and 5. to serve as a repository of sacred knowledge for future civilizations. The secrets of the pyramid-crystal synergetic relationship were well known to these cultures and put to use in the ways listed above and in additional modes that would challenge the imagination of modern man.

Reflections of this knowledge are echoed in the wisdom of archetypal mythology:

Deeper and deeper I descended, drawn by some unknown energy towards a chamber in the very heart of the pyramid. In this mysterious room was a magnificent crystal sphere with gold coils in it. . . . As High Priestess I had studied this very crystal, understood its receiving powers, learned to transmit its energies, knew the secret of its light . . . "What are the gold coils in this one?" I indicated the glittering sphere above us. . . . "Coils of electrical energy. As Priestess, you knew how to channel the sun's energy in your crystal and send it throughout your working chambers. . . . Combine the sun's energy with powerful thoughts and anything can be created. For those who are trained and disciplined, there is nothing that cannot be called into being or removed from the physical plane."[23]

Age-old memories are also surfacing in glimpses of remembrance:

. . . [C]ould these present-day scientists have been duplicating from a psychic memory, that which they saw and helped destroy in ancient Atlantis? The power beams which emerged from the Atlantis pyramid were intercepted by similar metallic rods of crystallized metal which, because they oscillated in a similar manner and frequency, presenting no resistance to the power of the beam. The beam then travelled straight through the rod or was broken up and separated into separate beams by a crystal prism. . . . In utilizing these power beams in a dwelling, a metal ball fitted on top of a metal rod, like a small flagpole, contained a crystal of certain prismatic configurations which directed the beam down through the hollow center . . . so that the round milky-white crystal globes would go glowing with light, motors turn, etc.[24]

A trickle of the hidden technological treasures referred to in many prophecies is also emerging. Dr. Ray Brown of Mesa, Arizona, for example, reports that while doing extensive scuba diving in the Bermuda Triangle, he located and entered a large underwater pyramid of large dimensions. While inside he found a 2½-inch diameter crystal ball with four aligned pyramidal shapes within it. This crystal has undergone extensive testing and its precise characteristics are difficult to determine, as the energies within and around it fluctuate widely and unpredictably. It is reported to glow internally and to emanate powerful energy fields at various times. A photograph of an eye inside the crystal ball has been taken. Some have theorized that it is an electro-optical interdimensional communication device that has yet to be fully reactivated into functioning. It is also postulated that this crystal and the pyramid in which it was found were part of the once extant worldwide system of pyramid-crystal energy generators. When intense geological disturbances occurred, thrusting many land masses underwater, the precise harmonic balance of the whole network became disrupted. This crystal ball and other key crystals yet to be found will play a crucial role in re-establishing this global energy network.[25]

Another unique and enigmatic discovery occurred in 1927 when the explorer-archeologist F. A. Mitchell-Hedges led an expedition to some ancient Mayan ruins. There, it is reported that he found a large crystal shaped into the form of a human skull. A number of unusual phenomenon have been observed by Frank Dorland, a "bio-crystallographer" in Los Osos, California. Over a period of 5 years, many striking phenomenon were observed, including 1. visible changes in color and transparency and an appearance of images, some of which have been photographed; 2. the giving off of an unmistakable scent; 3. sounds of chanting and tinkling silver bells; and 4. dramatic physical changes in people who have been in close proximity. It is theorized that it was formed through the thought projections of a group of seven Mayan priests and that the crystal skull functioned as a receptor for knowledge, wisdom, and guidance from the higher realms of Spirit.[26]

Much arcane knowledge and many technological devices have been hidden away and carefully guarded by the Spiritual Hierarchy of Light. As a new era of Earth's history unfolds, this spiritual treasure will be re-collected by selected people at the appropriate times. These divine technologies will be activated once again to fulfill their highest purpose. All over the world at specific locations—underwater, underground, in secret tunnels, in wilderness areas, and so on—our divine inheritance will arise like a phoenix from the ashes. The Cyclopeans, or Els, left valuable stores of information when they departed from the Earth-plane as a group.

. . . [G]reat libraries in their deep, underground empire of enormous cities. In these libraries tiny crystal records contain the history of the Universe, and are enclosed in a magnetic field which, at times, finds an affinity with some "sensitive" person living on Earth today."[27]

Edgar Cayce has channeled that many secrets of Atlantean crystal technology are located in three places—in the sunken portion of Atlantis, in Bimini (off the coast of Florida), and in the Yucatan in Mexico.[28] In the book *The Treasure of El Dorado*, Joseph Whitfield reports being taken to many of these secret chambers, among them a secret room in the Great Pyramid.

What you are about to see, Joseph, is how the Great Pyramid of Giza was constructed, and why. . . . I sat spellbound as the room darkened and the space in front of our chairs became alive with three-dimensional activity. The machine turned out to be a laser holographic projector. The holographic images were somehow stored in the crystal, and the laser projector was able to register the stored images and show them as a perfect three-dimensional movie.[29]

The Book of Knowledge: The Keys of Enoch, by J. J. Hurtak, reports that:

. . . [T]he secrets of the heavenly temples of YHWH coded into stone models and left behind in "holy dwelling places" of the Sons of Light as a beacon to higher Wisdom.[30]

. . . [A]t the end of this time cycle, there shall be scriptures of crystal found in the oceans and scriptures of stone found in the land of Yucatan, and scriptures of Light found throughout the world. . . .[31]

As many prophecies state, we are rapidly nearing the end of a time cycle, the Omega point of evolution, wherein man shall be transformed into the fourth-dimensional Light-body as the Earth, too, is totally remade and transmuted into higher octaves of Light. Crystal technologies play a key role as windows of Light as a New World dawns whereupon "man will walk over time like a bio-satellite moving over a crystalline staircase."[32]

Chapter 2

QUARTZ CRYSTALS

Seeds of Wholeness

"Wholeness: A Treatise"

There is but one atom, one seed that comprises the universe. It is on this premise that the subject of wholeness will be approached. This premise is not founded on man's law, but on God's law and divinity and it is for man to put in the perspective of his own thought pattern, for it is in these patterns that the law exists. For each man must abide by the patterns of his growth, both on physical as well as higher planes, such that all will be completed and known in time as the pattern is manifested in this soul existence. Is it not for each man to choose his own path so that it relates to the structure of the living universe?

To speak of wholeness, again we must return to the path of paths, the way of ways, the flow of flows, for all exists in accordance with this grand and elegant movement. Watch the stars as they spiral towards the infinite space, only to be absorbed by that space. So do men spiral at the same relative speed as the stars towards the infinite body of God—God the Father and Mother as one, the creator and the receiver at each end of the spiral, not to be confused with the God-head principle; the wholeness of the universe encompasses even this.

The very soul of the universe breathes the essence of the four elements (earth, wind, water, fire) and those other elements unknown to man. These four known elements are, in universally recognized terms: substance, antisubstance, flow, and energy; and the unknowns are projected into the minds of men in relation to the angles of their perceptual fields, which is another subject unto itself.

And it is within the blending of these inherent elementals that the primary transmutation of energy occurs and the birth of soul-matter receives its first Light, traveling the realms until it becomes one with the Light. Always it travels in precise geometric spirals, surrounded by illusionary worlds unknown by the Law or the Light. The union of souls in the Light causes the combustion of energy needed to perpetuate the cycle—endlessly, effortlessly, without attachment or detachment.

Thus it can be seen then that the soul's journey is not a chosen pattern, though the path is well chosen. The soul may shatter into a thousand or more particles to view or to experience the millions of creations within and around the spiral, many aspects of the same Light traveling along the universal pattern, merging as one as the spiraled point is drawn into the whole. And within this whole, all spirals exist and begin and end simultaneously and manifest themselves into all realms—a single breath.

Crystals are seeds of wholeness containing resonating blueprints of perfection that people may use to clarify their own unique spiral paths of wholeness. They are as resonating pathways of spiraling Light, connecting the Many Mansions of the Father's House. Throughout the wholeness of creation, we find our very own Self reflected within the infinite facets of living Crystal-Light. This Light *is* reality—there is nothing else. When the fiat was proclaimed, "Let there be Light," the Living Light shot forth at infinite speeds, manifesting a Whole-Light Synthesis within the limitless dimensions of the cosmos. Crystals, as messengers of Light, hold the keys to re-collecting our individual and collective "Song of the Heavens," our spiral evolutionary path of ascension into the higher realms of our divine heritage.

The Universal Mind, the I AM THAT I AM, pervades every particle of creation, thus inspiring each level of existence with Divine Intelligence. The universe, from each atom to the collective unity of the whole, can be aptly viewed as a great Mind, with each part being whole unto itself and at the same time each aspect partaking of the Whole-Light Synthesis of the All. The reflection of Divine Intelligence can be seen from the magnificent spiral patterns of supergalaxies to the complex dynamics of human evolution to the mathematically precise harmonics of the subatomic world. The microcosm and the macrocosm are as one; all levels reflect the Universal Mind through the crystal mirroring of wholeness throughout the infinite strata of manifestation. Truly, we live in a "many and one universe."[1]

As a facet of creation, quartz crystals reflect the Intelligence of the Universal Mind. As such, the quartz kingdom is a unique evolving life form.

Nullifying all preconceived ideas, it wouldn't be difficult to believe that gems have a soul, because, in the final analysis everything that exists must evolve according to a certain Intelligent Principle. . . .[2]

Indeed, crystals are as man, whose soul's journey is not a chosen pattern, though the path is well chosen. For crystals are to man as man is to crystals—children of Light, evolving, giving from one to the other, and finally merging into universal wholeness together.

The spiral evolutionary path of the quartz kingdom interfaces with that of the Earth in dynamic synergy. Viewing the Earth as a sentient being of a specific evolutionary order, commonly known as the Gaia hypothesis, its constituent components may be perceived as parts of a wholistic mind-body unity. Within this perspective, it could be seen that such primitive stone as granite and sandstone developed as the framework or skeleton, the Earth's crust congealed as the skin covering, and the vegetation grew as a breathing, nutrient-forming area. Water channels through aquifers, rivers, lakes, and oceans as the lifeblood of existence; the metals and minerals function as the glands, nerves, and sense organs; and man serves a conscious, intuitive-rational, cocreative function. Quartz crystals specifically act as a brain-mind through which the Universal Mind may maintain continual communication and continuity with the collective unity of the sentient Earth. Vast deposits of metals and gemstones permeate the globe's energy field, creating a unified electromagnetic field of life. Gemstones of the different rainbow rays serve as different facets of the Earth-mind. Quartz, the capstone of the physical plane, unifies the seven rainbow rays of the various gemstones and infuses the wholeness of the White Light throughout the Earth-being.

Crystalline order is the matrix of all life. A crystalline structure is one in which the atoms and molecules line up, sort themselves, and form repeating rows, layers, and lattices according to highly specific laws of harmonic order. This is the essence of "crystals"—the creation and maintenance of organization. Ordered solids—from rock, wood, and water to muscle, bone, and gene—are all describable as "crystal." Further, all levels of creation—from galaxies to man to atoms—can be viewed as organized Intelligence which is highly crystalline in nature. Each level of manifestation has its own unique order, and the evolutionary process is one in which a recrystallization occurs into a higher order of Intelligence. Thus, the order of the cosmos reflects the limitless crystalline facets of the Universal Mind.

Quartz, as one level of "crystal," has a set of unique properties and characteristics that make it a key living connection within and between all aspects of manifestation. All quartz is formed according to specific laws of crystalline growth. The chemical formula of pure quartz is SiO_2—one silicon atom linking two oxygen atoms to form a single bonded unit. According to the electromagnetic laws of repulsion and attraction, groups of SiO_2 molecules link with each other to form spirals of molecular units in a precise geometrical ratio, which together form a three-dimensional latticework of repeating, systematic uniformity. On the macroscopic level these molecular spirals form a crystal that has six sides, each one forming a 120-degree angle with the adjacent sides. Notice, too, that opposite sides are always parallel to one another. A seventeenth-century crystallographer, Nicolaus Steno, founded a fundamental scientific law when he realized through examining quartz crystals that despite their differences in size, shape, and origin, the angles between the corresponding faces are constant. This discovery set the stage for the study of all crystalline substances and is known today as Steno's Law. In fact, there are seven main systems of organization in the mineral kingdom. These seven "systems of symmetry" are defined by three or four imaginary axes of equal or unequal length that intersect at the center of any perfect, undistorted crystalline form. The lengths and number of the axes and the angles between them define a mineral's shape. The seven crystal systems are classified as cubic, hexagonal, rhombohedral, tetragonal, orthorhombic, monoclinic, and triclinic. Quartz crystal is of the hexagonal system that is defined by four axes, three of which are of equal length and lie in a plane with angles of 120 degrees between them; the fourth axis is perpendicular to the plane of the other three and may be of any length (see Figure 1). Thus it is within these parameters that the unvarying format of quartz exists.

The mineral kingdom reflects Divine Intelligence through both its exoteric and esoteric aspects. The exoteric facets are expressed through such physical characteristics as weight, hardness, and chemical composition, and the esoteric aspects are reflected in the geometry and mathematical relationships that occur on the microscopic and macroscopic levels. The seven crystal systems, then, are a mirroring of different facets of the Universal Mind and bear its codes of wholeness and perfection. As atoms of ''like-consciousness,'' or like-vibration, are attracted to one another and coalesce

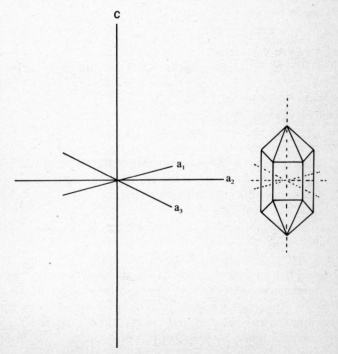

Figure 1: The Hexagonal Crystal System

into the various crystal systems, this results in an organized field of energy expressing a definite vibrational quality. This can be called the Law of Crystal Ordering—the tendency of like-vibrational atoms and molecules to gather together to form a specific and coherent vibratory whole. Within the dynamics of each distinct vibratory unit, the patterns of molecular forces and the resultant crystalline forms reflect the causal principles of the Universal Mind. Therefore, we can view "crystal" as a master code that, when completely known, can lead us toward higher levels of self-integration and transformation.

The angles and algebraic formulas involved in the various crystal systems are that which is important to the lesson that it teaches or the work that is done, for even as *all* things are "love," so are all things mathematically sound. As man is able to study these particular systems and relate them unto himself, he will more clearly see the workings of his *own* mind and body, and his own place within the universe.[3]

Within the spectrum of the seven crystal systems, it is the hexagonal system that includes the quartz crystal with which we are specifically concerned. On a metaphysical level, the physical crystal reflects man's inner crystalline nature; the outer crystal is a tool to reflect the inner Light. The hexagonal system, in this sense, is essentially one of dynamic equilibrium and balance. The three equal axes that lie in one plane are perfectly symmetrical in relationship to one another. The fourth axis is one of varying length that relates directly to the establishment of the mathematical relationships between the facets of the crystal. Thus the three axes in equilibrium have the added dimensions of the varying fourth axis through which an infinite number of potential expressions of dynamic balance and stability may be manifest. Within quartz, specifically, the molecular spirals exist within the general hexagonal system, creating a Light-attracting and Life-giving crystal structure. The spiral is a fundamental harmonic of all cosmic energies and as the crystal resonates with these energies, they are set in motion within the crystal, alchemically recrystallized within the patterns of equilibrium and balance, and released in a Life- and Light-transforming manner. So it is that two essential facets of cosmic order—the spiral and the hexagon—are combined into an archetypal model of the deeper meaning of giving and receiving.

The spiral molecular structure of quartz interfaces with that tiniest seed-blueprint of creation—DNA. The crystal lattices themselves serve as rudimentary "genes" in admitting only certain select molecules to fasten and grow upon them in precise ways. The smallest seed-crystal placed in a favorable medium will reproduce with undeviating accuracy the same crystal structure as it grows larger. The vast spiral networks of DNA, too, are very specific in the codes of life that they carry. As DNA replicates, its components will allow only certain "building blocks" of precise requirements to be attached. Thereby it creates a spiral crystalline latticework that closely resembles the molecule-specific crystal "genes" in its basic mode of functioning. It is possible that a crystalline mineral was life's first and simplest reproductive technique on Earth. (Recall Alexander Cairns-Smith's ideas on this topic that are presented in the Introduction.)

In their search for life in all this seemingly frozen abstraction, the crystallographers eventually settled on the spiral crystal as the probable ancestor or cousin of the helical molecules that compose all protein and genes.[4]

In shamanism, too, quartz crystal is likened to the very essence and repository of life.

. . . [B]one, like quartz crystal or seed, is the enduring source from which light and life spring anew. Shamans, like other religious ascetics, divest themselves of flesh, reduce their bodies to that mysterious yet durable matter, which, like the liquid crystal semen, is the fertile source, ever capable of reproducing itself, and, like the quartz crystal, is the clear body, the diamond body, the bone of emanant light. Bone, like a crystal or a seed, has a dual aspect and represents both the repository of the very source of life and that which is not perishable.[5]

DNA and quartz, spiral seed-blueprints of life, both serve to coordinate the development of life and the imprinting of Spirit into matter. And as we shall see in the following chapters, the functioning of both DNA and quartz are two aspects of the same function.

Light itself, manifests spirally, and its spiral motion is reflected in the solidified Light of crystals as a spiral molecular structure.

And through understanding the spiral nature of Light, we gain greater comprehension of the nature of quartz. Light is an actual transportation of energetic particles or "wave packets" through space via a dual-polarity, spiral oscillatory motion. Emanating from the still-point of the unmanifest, the Void, manifest Light combines the qualities of linear, forward movement—the straight line—with that of infinity—the circle. Together these two elements form a dynamic fusion yielding a spiral. The picture of electron tracks in a bubble chamber shows a direct analogy of this process. "Positive," masculine energies moving in a straight line are observed colliding with "negative," feminine energies moving in a circle. As they unite a spiral is created, inheriting the forward progress of the line while maintaining the conserving principle within its cyclic wave.

A beam of white light starts as a circle with dual polarity. The masculine and feminine or positive and negative or horizontal and vertical rays of this white light make the dual aspect, but it has to move forward; that makes the third aspect forming the Trinity. As a circle that moves forward forming a gyratory spiral, the white light therefore becomes a progressive spiral oscillatory motion with the dual polarity energy, kept in check by the third aspect. . . ."[6]

As Light crystallizes into the physical octave in the form of quartz, it retains the essential characteristics of Light and, as such, is exemplified through the universal symbol of Light, the Star of David.

It appears that the whole source, motion, and function of light can be contained in that mysterious hexagonal figure known as the Star of David. It has been pointed out that as an energy pattern this figure expresses a spiral.[7]

While the Star of David is generally known as a Judaic religious symbol, it is *also* a fundamental universal symbol of sacred geometry. The discussion above of the esoteric significance of the seven crystal symmetry systems in general and the hexagonal system in particular demonstrate how key mathematical relationships and geometric forms reflect aspects of the Universal Mind; and so it is with the Star of David. This timeless symbol is composed of two intersecting equilateral and equidistant triangles. The inverted triangle symbolizes the materialization of Spirit into matter, the yin principle, the earthly energies. The upright triangle symbolizes the ascension of matter into Spirit, the yang principle, the heavenly energies. As a whole, the Star of David represents a dynamic balance and union between these fundamental polarities of creation.

This figure is used to represent the "marriage" of the kundalini and the Primary Force. Two interlacing triangles, one descending, the other ascending, move toward a potential intersection at the heart chakra in the form of a hexagon. . . . This union or intersection creates the current which bears the light throughout the body.[8]

This marriage of Light occurs in man (whose numerological equivalent is six), manifesting as a state of dynamic equilibrium and balance between matter and Spirit, yin and yang, corresponding to the esoteric significance of the hexagonal system mentioned above.

Further, the quartz crystal merges with the Star of David energy pattern from a number of additional perspectives. First, notice that the equilateral three-axis component of the hexagonal crystal system is apparent in the Star of David if lines are drawn from each apex of the figure to the opposite apex. The angles between these three lines are identical to the corresponding aspect of the hexagonal crystal system (Figure 2A). The same effect can be produced by connecting the opposite corners of the hexagon created by the intersection of the two triangles (Figure 2B). Notice, too, that there are six triangles around the outer part of the Star of David. By folding them up towards each other along the axis of the inner hexagon, the form of a perfect quartz crystal is created—six top facets on a hexagonal base (Figure 2C). Within the hexagonal base of this crystal form, another Star of David can be created by connecting every other vertex (Figure 2D). It is now evident that each and every horizontal cross section of the crystal is infused with this universal symbol. In theory, then, there are an infinite number of Star of David patterns potentially existing within the crystal. The crystal form, therefore, both derives from and is infused with the Star of David geometry, and hence partakes of its symbolic properties. In fact, the crystal adds a physical dimension to the Star of David through its three-dimensionality and a metaphysical dimension by incorporating this geometrically activating

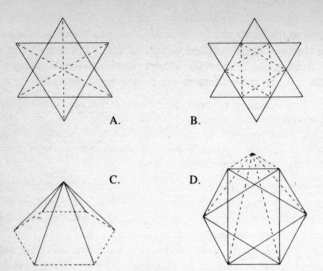

Figure 2: Sacred Geometry of the Star of David within Quartz Crystal's Structure

principle throughout each and every level of its structure. The potent synergy so created endows the crystal with the properties of dynamic union, balance, and harmony. The crystal now translates into a three-dimensional mandala of universal Light.

From another perspective of sacred geometry, consider the six facets of the crystal that converge to a single point—the still-point of Spirit—and the six surrounding facets as manifest angular emanations from the One. Six plus one yields seven, the fundamental harmonic of creation, a number of completion and perfection.

Six points are seen in the star, but the seventh cannot be seen; nevertheless, the seventh point must exist, although it has not become manifest; because without a center there could be no six-pointed star, or any other figure existing . . . the enlightened sees in that invisible center the Great Spiritual Sun, the heart of the Cosmos, from which Love and Light and Life are radiating forever.[9]

Crystals are the "eyes" of Spirit looking into matter and calling us back to the Source; they are born of the stars, planted in the Earth, and reborn through the rainbow. The Light of the heavens is infused into the Earth, there to connect the realms of Spirit and matter through the spiral rainbow staircase. Recall the source of crystals in shamanic cosmology as being "thrown" or brought down from the Otherworlds, there to serve as a living connection between dimensions. Quartz appeared the same to the shamans whether they were in an ecstatic trance or not; the material and spiritual nature of the crystal were perceived to be one and the same. Indeed, quartz is an "inexhaustible cosmic mine"[10] and transmission center of pure White Light, the manifestation of the universal Father Principle.

Spiritually, the White Light is the Divine Radiance of the Father of the Cosmos—the Logos. It is the Light of Christ-Consciousness, of Supreme Power, Purity, Perfection—the Primary Healing Power. It is the Light of At-One-Ment with the Source of Life.[11]

The White Light embodied in the quartz crystal unifies the manifest rays of the rainbow, fuses them in the Light of At-One-Ment, and thereby functions as a doorway to the higher realms of Light.

As White Light passes through quartz, a series of events occur in which the Light is dispersed into its spectral color components and then reconstituted back into white once again. The moment that Light enters a denser medium, it slows down and refracts, or bends. This is the phenomenon observed when a stick, for example, is placed half in and half out of water. There is a uniform and predictable refraction of the Light as it enters the water, making a straight stick appear to be bent. This same phenomenon happens in quartz. As Light enters the crystal, it is bent at a precise angle, called the refractive index, and disperses into the spectrum of colors. Basically, this is due to a difference in the amount that each color is bent. The colors with the longest wavelengths—those toward the red end—are refracted the least while those with the shorter wavelengths—those toward the violet end—are bent the most. This is exactly what occurs through a standard prism, i.e., it takes White Light into its structure and emits the rainbow spectrum out the other side. In the case of quartz, though, this phenomenon happens totally within the crystal itself. And as the incoming Light-rays refract, the resulting color spectrums merge and blend with each other, producing a net effect of White Light emerging out the other side of the crystal. In effect, what one Light-ray loses as it refracts is gained from the other Light-rays. Thus the crystal serves to both separate White Light and then to recombine its components back together.

Herein lies the basic dynamics for many aspects of the crystal's functions. It is within the complexities of this process as the color spectrums interface with the molecular structure of quartz that many technical aspects of crystal activities can be understood. Because quartz *is* crystallized White Light, it is more fully able than other minerals to resonate with interdimensional octaves of White Light. Each and every molecular unit of the crystal functions as an interdimensional membrane, or gateway, for the higher octaves of color to resonate and interact with the ''three-dimensional'' color octave. This is analogous to the difference between striking one note of C on a piano versus striking all octaves of C at once. In the latter instance, the vibrations interact much more strongly with each other due to the principle of harmonic resonance, thereby increasing the power and range of vibrations that intersect at each and every note (or nodal point) of C. Therefore, ''three-dimensional'' color can be potentiated—that is, made more powerful and whole—through a more direct resonant linkage with the higher octaves of color that exist on the more elevated celestial dimensions. Crystals, then, are as alchemical crucibles in which and through which the wholeness of White Light can be recrystallized into another appropriate wholistic format. Herein lies the key to interdimensional communication.

These crystal dynamics are a microcosmic image that points toward their macrocosmic functions.

Divine plan has foreordained that all expanding life revolve around one common denominator, quartz crystal. Through frozen solidified light all creation could be monitored and assisted through the evolutionary process.[12]

On the cosmic levels, crystals serve as separator and balancer. Separation occurs so that consciousness can be reconstituted into another level of wholistic balance. All aspects of creation are constantly changing, and therefore the element of a continual balancing factor is very crucial to the stability and maintenance of Divine Order. Many other agents contribute in various ways to cosmic balance and cohesion, but it is the crystal that is the primary facilitator for the vast task of intercommunication between all levels of manifestation. The word *communication* is used here in the broadest sense—communication of the full spectrum of energy interactions so that a dynamic, homeostatic balance may be maintained within and between the infinite dimensions of the Universal Mind. And, as we shall see in the next chapter, this task is a most technologically advanced one that requires great knowledge of the mathematical order of the cosmos and of how crystals can be used as repositories of vibrational codes and as intelligent modulators and balancers. Taken to its logical conclusion, unlimited and instantaneous interdimensional communication merges into spiritual communion—at-one-ment with the Universal Mind. As the cornerstone of Divine Order, the wholeness of the quartz crystal indeed unites the Alpha with the Omega, the low with the high, the Earth with the Heavens.

Chapter 3

TECHNOLOGICAL PERSPECTIVES

Communication as a Cornerstone of Scientific and Consciousness Transformations

The evolutionary process is one of realizing the essential keynote of communication, or "communion," within and between all levels of creation. As every being evolves, the communicative capacity is heightened along with the awareness of its importance. Through this process an increasing recognition of the Divine Intelligence within every unit of consciousness unfolds and produces a growing rapport with the Universal Mind. Communication, in the broadest sense of the word, is the process of distributing the ever-unfolding, ever-expanding flow of Love and Light throughout all manifestation. Through the sharing in this flow via increasing angles of perception, the evolving soul partakes of expanding degrees of the informational context of the Whole. All information, all communication within the Universal Mind is whole, or spherical, in nature. The larger the angle of the soul's perceptual field, the greater the degree of the Divine communication matrix received. Full communication or "communion" yields at-one-ment, or a spherical perceptual field resonating within every atom existing throughout the infinity of creation. To achieve such a state is to attain total self-realization, or cosmic consciousness.

Crystals are a quintessential medium of communication. As capacitors of the full spectrum of Sound and Light, they serve as angular receivers, modifiers, regulators, and projectors of the spherical information emanations of Divine Intelligence. For man, crystals can be used as a means of expanding the perceptual field to greater degrees in order to encompass higher octaves, or "spherical quotients," of information. The higher the octave of energy, the larger the angular projection; and as man increases his field of perception, the "lines" of communication open up to encompass increasing degrees of the spherical "thoughts" of the Universal Mind. Through the precise angular relationships existing within a crystal, the spherical information quanta are decoded, or modulated, into specific angular energy patterns of information according to the mathematical relationships of the crystal's angles and molecular structure. In their higher octaves of use, crystals can increase an individual's perceptual field to contain the precise angular harmonies of the crystal, thus providing a meeting ground, or "communication chamber," between the various intra- and interdimensional spherical energy patterns.

Crystals, as they are used in present-day forms of communication technologies, reflect a growing awareness of the higher octaves of crystal technology. Currently, they are integral elements of some of man's most sophisticated inventions. From computers and photovoltaics to watches and radio transmitters, crystals and their human-made variations are used as components of reception, regulation, modulation, storage, and transmission of electromagnetic energies. We live today within a matrix of crystal technologies that have played a key role in making this "age of communication" possible. Mankind's collective angle of perception has grown by quantum leaps in the twentieth century as the communication networks of such inventions as radio, television, and computers have increased the ability to transfer information over great distances with lightning speed and efficiency. Within 10 years from today it is projected that computer-based technologies will give instantaneous access to information on a worldwide basis to each individual from a computer in the home and office. Mankind will then make another significant advance as the world is linked together through a collective "electronic brain." And, as a new era of consciousness transformation unfolds, even greater degrees of collective, communicative communion will occur, catalyzed through developments in the Divine Science of the future.

One of the primary properties for which quartz is valued in modern-day science is termed the piezoelectric effect. This property was discovered in 1880 by Pierre and Jacques Curie, who also discovered radium, as they were studying the electrical conductivity of crystalline substances. In measuring the conductivity of quartz, they observed that pressure on the test plates produced a measurement on a sensitive electrometer (a device that measures electric-potential differences). The piezoelectric effect is a twofold phenomenon—mechanical pressure on a crystal will produce a measurable voltage, and conversely, an electrical voltage applied to a crystal will produce mechanical movement. The natural resonant frequency of the crystal plate (a cross section cut from a crystal) is determined primarily by its thickness and size. As either pressure or electricity is applied, opposite charges develop on alternate prismatic sides. When an alternating electrical current is passed through the crystal plate, the charges oscillate back and forth at the resonant frequency of the crystal. This is the basis for the crystal-oscillator components used in electronics to generate, maintain, and stabilize very precise energy frequencies. For example, radio and television stations must send out their signals on a well-defined frequency, and it is the crystal oscillator that is the key to maintaining this vibration within exact limits. On the other hand, the crystal's ability to convert, or transduce, mechanical stress into voltage is used in a different way. For example, a phonograph needle connected to a crystal element rides in the grooved patterns in a record. As the needle is forced back and forth by the fluctuations of the groove, various mechanical stresses are transferred to the crystal that are then converted to an electrical signal that can be amplified and processed by the other elements of the circuitry, the end result being sound projected through the speaker system. Thus, the crystal's marked ability to function as a stabilizer and transducer makes it a key component in such devices as watches, heaters, ultrasonic devices, radar, sonar, microphones, radio, television, telemetry devices, telecommunication technology, and numerous others.

While quartz plates are a key aspect of electrical devices, it is the element of silicon itself that is a very important medium in the field of solid-state electronics. This area of technology concerns the electrical dynamics that occur in solid materials and is the basis for the "silicon revolution" of computer technology. The rapidly increasing sophistication in the realms of artificial intelligence, robotics, computers, and video games is based on the information-storing capabilities of elemental silicon. Basically, silicon is a semiconductor, a material that has intermediate qualities between an insulator (little or no electrical conductivity) and a conductor (readily transfers electricity). In order for silicon to transfer an electrical charge, the charge must be strong enough to "push" an electron free from the atom so that it can flow in an electrical current. It is this capacity to either retain an electrical charge or not, according to the amount of energy input, that is the basis for computer memory. Computers work on a binary basis; that is, there are two basic elements that serve as the basis for all computer operations— 0 or 1, yes or no, on or off. Each silicon chip, usually about 1 centimeter square and ½ millimeter thick, contains hundreds of thousands of tiny transistors, each one being simply on or off, charged or not charged. Taken together as a whole, these transistors translate into numbers, words, and functions. Simply stated, then, this is the basis of computer technology—the semiconducting properties of silicon that can be precisely regulated on microscopic levels.

Solar energy devices also use silicon as a primary element. In this case, it is employed for its ability to convert solar Light-energy into an electrical current. This process is known as the photoelectric effect and occurs as incoming light is absorbed by the silicon, adding energy and thereby setting electrons free to flow in an electrical current. Metal conductors collect this current and transfer it to be used in the same way that "regular" electricity is utilized.

It is important to note here that in both computer and solar technologies it is elemental silicon (Si) that is used as a primary component, *not* natural quartz (SiO_2). Today's science uses laboratory-purified elemental silicon as the fundamental substratum in which to infuse, or "dope," other select elements. Very small but extremely precise amounts of these other elements are doped into a crystal as it grows in the laboratory. Each doping element will, in conjunction with the surrounding matrix of silicon, produce very precise degrees of electrical conductivity, optical activity, thermal conductivity, and a host of other calibrated properties. This is a highly sophisticated science that the crystallographers have expressed in many volumes of information. The main point here is that while natural quartz is utilized in much of electronics, scientists have also created a wide variety of silicon-based crystalline substances that form the basis of key modern technologies. Especially in the field of computers, we see a technology that many experts foresee changing the very fabric of modern civilization within the next ten to twenty years. It is the authors' perspective that the Divine Science of the future will show that natural quartz crystal will be the primary basis for all communication, computer, and energy-related technologies. The scientists of today have not yet fully understood the holistic Light-properties of natural quartz and because of this have developed laboratory-produced quartz *variations* that will eventually evolve into knowledge concerning the holographically-based interdimensional energy access that quartz affords. From an evolutionary perspective, we can see that present-day science has explored many of the potential applications of quartz-based technologies in a relatively linear fashion that is already proving in some fields to be a limiting factor toward future innovative developments. When a Divine Science unlocks the technical mysteries of natural quartz with divinely inspired "keys," quantum technological advancements will occur within the patterns of crystalline Light.

In this brief overview, then, it can be seen that the key function of the crystal-based technologies of today is communication—the dissemination of organized energies from one location to another, be it light, voice, electricity, information, or ultrasound. These instruments have generated a prodigious leap in both the amount of available information and the ways to communicate in more sophisticated and encompassing ways. Such advancements are continuing today in the high-tech world at an even more rapid pace than before. Indeed, we are on the threshold of an era wherein high technology will restructure the very fabric of society. And, as with all powerful forces, there is a double-edged sword inherent in the progress of science. These advances can be used for constructive and uplifting purposes or for harmful and aberrant ends, as in Atlantis. The *key* is to join spiritual insight and wisdom with scientific research and development. It is partially a matter of ethical principles, to be sure; however, spiritual knowledge brings with it, too, a deeper cognition of the precise harmonics of a highly complex, multidimensional creation. A larger "sphere of perception" brings knowledge that can be practically applied in a scientific manner. The blending of the Universal Mind with science is one means of uniting the Heavens with the Earth. As mankind progresses into this realization, we shall see the crystal-based technologies of today blossom forth into fruition through Divine Science. Within these Light-based technologies of tomorrow, the quartz crystal is a wholistic seed-crystal around which all else crystallizes. Let us explore in the following pages some glimpses into these windows of Light.

The Divine Science of crystal energetics is essentially one of harnessing the primary power of living Light and modifying it for multiple applications. The prepotent force of the higher octaves of Light is truly awesome, dimly echoed in the brightness and raw energy of the Sun. The crystallized Light of quartz has these magnitudes of dynamic energy inherent within its structure. One such example of this reality lies in the tradition of central California Indian shamans who would periodically "wake up" certain large "parent" crystals. It was done by striking the crystal as hard as possible on a specific rock a few feet offshore in the Pacific Ocean. This procedure was considered to be a very dangerous one, for if the crystal shattered, it was believed that the world would end. Almost certainly, this belief is not true on a worldwide basis but may be a very accurate description of what could happen on an individual basis.

A well-known physicist, David Finkelstein, on hearing of this belief, remarked that the death of the shaman would have been quite possible. He stated that striking such a large quartz crystal a smashing blow theoretically could release hundreds of thousands of volts, or sufficient energy to electrocute the medicine man. Western science has obviously advanced to the point that it recognizes the quartz crystal as a power object, something that shamans have known for thousands of years.[1]

Another example concerns an earthquake that occurred on November 19, 1930, in Japan in an area of a lava field containing quartz. It was accompanied by spectacular lightning in a clear sky:

. . . [A] phenomenon already becoming well enough recognized to have disseminated the theory that piezoelectric crystal subjected to disruptive mechanical pressure over many square miles of territory can generate voltage sufficient to cause a thunderstorm.[2]

The potential voltage that lies within quartz is indeed enormous, for as the "frozen" Light is activated and released, a glimpse of the power of the higher realms flashes on Earth.

Piezoelectricity is actually only one octave of the phenomenon of electricity. The Universal Mind, and all Intelligence within it, encompassing the realms of the supergalactic to the human to the subatomic, all function within the matrix of the total spectrum of electricity. Essentially, electricity is a fundamental harmonic of polar opposites of Light. It is analogous to the creation of the oppositely charged surfaces that oscillate from side to side in a crystal, except on a more macrocosmic level. Every level of manifestation is interconnected through the living Light of the harmonic octaves of electricity. As such, it is a living, conscious medium, a form of underlying Intelligence. This basic concept is echoed by Nobel laureate Albert Szent-Gyorgyi:

The fuel of life is the electron or, more exactly, the energy it takes over from photons in photosynthesis; this energy the electron gives up gradually while flowing through the cellular machinery.[3]

The scientist-philosopher Guy Murchie goes further in his observations:

In sum, it now appears almost certain that piezoelectricity is a common attribute of tissues, working unobtrusively not only in much of the mineral kingdom but in virtually all of the vegetable and animal kingdoms. And accumulating evidence strongly hints that senses in every kingdom operate more or less piezoelectrically, probably including still undeveloped ones.[4]

The functioning of the human bio-energetic system has been confirmed through research as being electromagnetic in nature. The noted researchers Albert Roy Davis and Walter C. Rawls conclude:

In this . . . outline of the bioelectrical potential found to exist in man there is evidence of human electrical and electromagnetic aura. The entire body of man is a field of continuing flowing electromagnetic energy, and the space emissions of this form of energy have been recorded.[5]

Beyond the aspects of electricity already known, there are multitudes of octaves that have yet to be totally understood. Psi energies, for example, are another octave of electricity through which a number of man's higher faculties operate, such as clairvoyance, clairaudience, telepathy, and remote viewing. William Tiller, head of the materials science department at Stanford, asserts that these kinds of extrasensory abilities take place in "negative space-time," a realm in which "magnetoelectric" energies travel at 10^{10} times the speed of physical-octave light.[6] Even higher octaves are the primary frequencies for other forms of spiritual intelligence, which include thought-form technologies, spectral Light-linguistics, Light-transmissions, and many more to be understood later in the evolutionary sequence. Quartz, in this regard, is an electrical tool that acts as a lightning rod and crucible through which we have greater access to the various levels of electricity.

Magnetics, on the other hand, is the science of conditional polarization. Within the dynamics of duality, opposite poles organize the fundamental coordinates for the interactions between all energies. As the unmanifest becomes manifest, the "latent" energy is activated—opposite poles manifest as the "negative" and the "positive" aspects of duality, and these magnetic poles serve as an intelligent organizing field in which electricity is maintained and modulated according to myriad variables. The important point here is that the magnetic element of creation manifests a unified field wherein the dynamics of Divine Intelligence occur. The noted spiritual scientist Walter Russell states:

That which man calls matter, or substance, has no existence whatsoever. So-called matter is but waves of the motion of light, electrically conditioned and patterned into what we call various substances of matter. Matter is but the motion of light, and motion is not substance. It only appears to be. Take motion away and there would not even be the appearance of substance.

Electricity manufactures all the qualities and attributes of light in wave motion which we think of as substance. All qualities and even appearance is given to waves of light by the two electrical workers which build up the universe and tear it apart in polarized fields measured out by the two magnetic surveyors which keep all electric actions in balance with their reactions.[7]

Through the modification of magnetic variables, the "playground" of electricity is altered to create precise coordinate patterns. The healing of the physical body, for example, can be attained through appropriate adjustments of the electromagnetic fields in which "matter" has its existence. Proper application of these precise energy fields in this respect may be called the harmonics of health. By adjusting the etheric organizing field of tissues, organs, glands, and so on, the physiological functioning harmonizes with the more causal vibratory patterns. Within every level of every energy field of creation, magnetics creates the fundamental coordinates in which each unit of consciousness functions.

Crystals, from this perspective, contain the code patterns of the electromagnetic (and gravitic) coordinates of Light-frequencies as they crystallize into the form of quartz. The molecular latticework holds this information code steady and functions as a "seed of wholeness" that can be stimulated in order to activate powerful force fields of specific parameters. This is basically a matter of activating the code patterns and extending them through the environment, thus recrystallizing the electromagnetic fields. The Oraxians and Atlanteans, for example, created energy domes that covered thousands of square miles. This aspect of crystal technology, then, is essentially the science of applied holistic energetics.

The Universal Mind manifests in Divine Order—a highly precise, efficient, and mathematically based mode of continual creation. The Whole-Light Synthesis forms multidimensional gridworks, or lattices, that contain the essential patterns of evolutionary growth dynamics. The Power of the Source reverberates interdimensionally through various "gates," or portals, whereby Light is patterned and transduced spirally. And as Light flows from octave to octave, it follows the patterns of the gridworks that are encoded at interdimensional membrane areas. Crystals serve as the main repositories and transmitters of these "genetic" codes. They are termed *template recorder cells* and their function is to hold complex coding sequences within their Light-based DNA structure. It is through such crystals that the DNA blueprint for each successive level of reality is recorded, maintained, and projected. As Light is transmitted from one dimension to another, it is modulated or recombined according to the Light-coding of the specific crystal through which it passes. As these patterns are reproduced and projected, they form the latticework of crystallization for the macrocosmic and microcosmic levels of each octave of creation. The DNA of the physical body, for example, is the crystallization of the primary patterns from code crystals of higher-dimensional frequencies. It is then through the procedure of DNA replication and transference that the physical body is patterned. The information transmitted through physical DNA reflects an analogous process that occurs on the cosmic levels. The key to multidimensional Light-transmittance is to align the membrane gateways so that the living Light may be channeled through to all the myriad facets of manifestation. In the midst of continual change, the Divine Image within each consciousness cell must be continually energized through the influx of the "manna" of appropriately coded Light.

Through the crystalline lattices, the Higher Evolution controls the various biological kingdoms by organizing the intergravitational and interradiational effects of lattice merging with lattice.[8]

Thus, the Whole-Light Synthesis recreates itself at each moment in the Now through the multidimensional "windows" of crystal template recorder cells.

The DNA grid structure of crystals is contained within the spiral molecular energy patterns in relationship to the specific angular configuration. The interaction of incoming Light-energies through the external faceting, spiral DNA structure, and internal optical activity creates a complex and precise interference pattern. The crystal, in effect, is a three-dimensional holographic interference plate that transfers its holographically based codes onto incoming Light. Going further into the dynamics of this process, we find that the *moment of refraction* plays an integral role. This is the exact moment of acceleration and bending of a Light-ray as it enters a crystal. The acceleration creates an alchemical fusion process wherein the Light is transmuted into a different quantum order. These fusion products are then bent, or refracted, into their spectral components at precise angles. As this spectrum travels through the crystal, it interfaces with the coded molecular patterns and is reflected at specific angles within the crystal according to optical principles. Amidst this whole basic process, certain principles allow modifications to occur. One means of such alteration is through varying the angle of the incoming ray so that it will be refracted to a different portion of the crystal. This means that the interference pattern that is created with reflect altered optical activity and angle of intersection with the DNA code patterns. Therefore, through minute adjustments of the incoming angle of projection, access to an infinite number of variations of intracrystal activity occurs. Through a sophisticated orchestration of varied angles, complex series of thought-forms and coding sequences can be generated. That is to say, each differing angle will produce a corresponding change in the interference pattern, and therefore a different holographic "message" will be created. This procedure is somewhat similar to the holographic movies of today's leading-edge technology. Another mode of variation is through the *malleability of moments*. This property is based upon the principle that the moment of refraction correlates directly with the speed of the incoming Light-ray. Basically, the element of speed alters both the amount of acceleration and the angle of the refracted fusion products. This creates even further means of modulating the internal crystal activity and thereby the resultant interference pattern. Thus the crystal serves as a highly complex holographic computer able to perform sophisticated Light-computations.

Another related characteristic of crystal energetics is called the *secondary refractive index*, which concerns the multiple-Light effect produced by the secondary reflection and refraction of Light within and around the crystal. This may be observed as the "aura"—a latticework of the color-sound "by-products" on the astral level that emanate from the primary Light-interactions discussed in the above paragraph. As such, this aspect directly reflects the nature of how the crystal is being used and the quality and intensity of the primary energy dynamics. This property can be used to monitor the crystal to gain feedback as to the integrity of the internal DNA coding and possible imbalances in the Light-interactions. And, as will be discussed below, the secondary refractive index can function in the monitoring, stabilizing, and healing of the human astral body.

The *transpositional quotient* is the linear processing of Light-interactions according to basic modulation and amplification quotients. This is a qualitatively different type of energy dynamic from the moment of refraction. The latter function is concerned with speeds of Light at or above the *critical mass*—the point of alchemical fusion producing a quantum change. It is the element of acceleration in the moment of refraction that produces the speed of Light required for alchemical fusion. The fusion products are then refracted into the interior of the crystal. Conversely, the transpositional quotient pertains to speeds of Light below the critical mass, and this involves basic modifications of Light without quantum change. Therefore, this level of energy interactions is of a less complex nature than those of the moment of refraction due to its relatively linear nature.

The process of *alchemical transfusion* is one of directing the Light-codes produced through the moment of refraction to their intended destination. This is done first by focalizing the fusion products into an appropriately prepared grid system of secondary crystals. As these fusion products are so collected, they are redirected along certain intra- and interdimensional pathways as programmed in the crystal gridwork. A similar procedure is used for the products of the transpositional quotient. In this case, too, the holographic codes are directed into a secondary crystal grid and directed to specific intradimensional locations. Basically, the only differences between these two modes are in the programming of the secondary crystals to take into account the more complex energy dynamics of the fusion products and their ability to be transfused both inter- and intradimensionally; the transfer of transpositional quotient products generally only occurs within a single dimensional plane.

Throughout the infinite cosmic dimensions, transference of communication is effected through continually changing, though constantly harmonic, resonating pathways of energy transmission. This multidimensional gridwork connects the myriad octaves of Light through the crystalline lattice lines that are determined by the programming of crystal template recorder cells in conjunction with the pyramidal form. The union of these two primary thought-forms of the Universal Mind functions as an *astrochronomic computer* set at key interdimensional vortexes, or energy-intersection areas. This pyramid-crystal unity functions synergistically as a complex computer that contains all potential functions and interactions of Light; it is both a repository and computation mechanism for every possible combination and permutation of Divine Intelligence. As a sophisticated and distinct level of consciousness—a living computer—it is the pinnacle of the interface between "artificial intelligence" and "living Intelligence." Indeed, it is a higher-octave example of the "living geometric forms" on which Pythagoras expounded in ancient history. Such a computer can receive and process instructions from various Light-beings and can also monitor and adjust a wide spectrum of intra- and interdimensional functions according to its basic programming. The nature of its "thoughts" are such that it can intelligently reprogram itself within certain parameters and can creatively modify projected instructions within its overall programming. Unlike any computer on Earth today, these living computers are composed of spherical units of consciousness that operate in a supraholographic manner and are able to receive and process billions of multiplexed "thoughts" instantaneously. From an overall perspective, the primary pyramid-crystal units are an aspect of the Universal Mind in one of its first levels of manifestation from the unmanifest. A whole unto itself and a jewel of Divine Intelligence, astrochronomic computers are primary seed-crystals of creation.

These Light-computers are related to gridworks of crystal template recorder cells existing at other harmonic points along the multidimensional lattice network as a computer is related to a computer terminal at another location. The crystal "terminal" receives the readout of the main computer and performs the functions of appropriately coded Light-interactions. The resulting readout is then transferred to other crystals or secondary astrochronomic computers, where it is processed and sent in sequential series through the crystalline latticework of each octave of manifestation.

Thus the "machinery" of the Universal Mind is set, and so it functions.

From perceptual-field modifiers to present-day electronics to cosmic computers, the keynote of crystal use is communication, or "communion." The progression of the current state of science into Divine Science will occur essentially through an upliftment of consciousness to encompass increasing degrees of interdimensional communication. Quartz crystals will be found to be one of the major unifying elements within quantum-field dynamics—the physics of the subatomic world—thus setting the stage for an era of multidimensional exploration that will exceed outer-space exploration in its ramifications. As physics moves to a unified field paradigm, the science of harmonics in conjunction with the nonlinear properties of crystals at very high- and extremely low-energy frequencies will show the way towards the realignment of the Earth's electromagnetic and gravitational field with higher-octave dimensional membrane areas. This will open the lines of communication with many other star systems and Light-dimensions as well as creating lattice lines that will be able to carry energies of a grand order to be used in myriad ways by Light-based technologies. These and other quantum advancements will be initiated with startling rapidity by the interfacing of high technology with the regaining of key technical information regarding the uniquely ''transparent'' properties of crystals. These crystal-based technologies will catalyze a collective elevation of consciousness leading to a future world based upon the principles of spiritual wisdom united with scientific technology. It is then that the Light of the Earth and the Heavens will be one and the same, as this world fulfills its destiny as an emerald of the celestial realms.

Chapter 4

THE CRYSTAL CHAKRAS

A New Perspective on the Human Energy System

Amid the duality of manifest creation, wholeness pervades the all-encompassing matrix of the Universal Mind. The negative and positive poles of manifestation are the bride and bridegroom ever moving through upward spirals of Divine union. Within the Alpha and the Omega, the beginning and the end of each cycle of the spiral evolutionary path, lies the seed-blueprint of the perfection and wholeness of the entire cycle. As above, so below; and so it is within the human chakra system. Above and below the negative pole of the coccyx (1st) center and the positive pole of the crown (7th) center, there exists the Alpha and Omega crystal chakras that hold the patterns of wholeness within human consciousness evolution. As an era of consciousness transformation dawns, mankind leaps forth from the Alpha stepping-stone of crystal through the Omega crystal capstone into the higher-octave chakra system of the Light-body.

For many centuries, the human bio-energetic system has been conceived of as seven major energy vortexes, consisting of centers located at the coccyx, splenic area, solar plexus, heart, throat, forehead, and crown. As a new world unfolds, supplemental divinely inspired knowledge comes forth to aid in the further development of Spirit-based healing perspectives. Much of this knowledge will bridge the gap between physics, metaphysics, and holistic health and will unite them into a Divine Meta-Science that will key a quantum transmutational process. As we approach the evolutionary Omega point, the uniting of the positive and negative polarities into a Whole-Light Synthesis on the next octave of existence occurs. This metamorphosis takes place within the fundamental cosmic harmonics of the quartz crystal and the double-pyramidal octahedron. Within the human bio-energetic system these harmonic geometries manifest as the crystal chakra existing on the Alpha energy frequency below the coccyx chakra and the pyramid with crystal capstone existing on the Omega energy level above the crown chakra. As seeds of wholeness, these crystal chakras are a key to the union of the seven chakras existing in polarity.

All life processes from the minute hydrogen atoms to the largest stellar formations resonate with the pyramid as the central geometric form for all biophysical and consciousness evolution. Universal Mind, energized in pyramidal harmonics, is present in every molecule of star ionization and every vibration of consciousness flow.

The keys to the living biophysical and astrophysical universe are the living "Light Pyramids of Life" existing within every structure within every field of creation.[1]

Divine Intelligence uses this structure as a unified interdimensional meeting ground that contains an infinite number of potential gridwork lattices that can be selectively activated to unite, modify, transmute, and transpose the myriad frequencies and levels of manifestation. At each evolutionary Omega point, consciousness must pass through a Pyramid of Light as it is recrystallized on a higher Light-dimension. Pyramidal frequencies are generated through the "Eye of Yahweh" in the center of the octahedron. This is the point of energization, communication, and reprogramming between interdimensional octaves. In conjunction with these dynamics, quartz crystals are positioned at key energy intersections and function as primary regulators of the Light-interactions. Together, the pyramid-crystal synergy creates a cosmic temple of continual creation and communication that resonates with ". . . the Million Myriads of Pyramids all interrelated into the Throne of the Divine."[2]

The Great Pyramid at Giza, in particular, is the "capstone" of all the numerous pyramids that dot the entire world at major energy vortexes. It is the Earth's primary "Pyramid of Light" that both balances and unites the whole global energy grid-system and holds many of the principle codes of Higher Intelligence. In connection with an inverted pyramid mirrored underneath the earth, this grand structure forms an octahedral shape.[3]

From this central focal point there is a network of magnetic resonance which connects all of the pyramidal energy fields around the Earth into a relationship of an icosahedron. This icosahedron grid is a monolithic structure of interlocking tetrahedrons and octahedrons which give the true harmonic reciprocals of Light acting on all points of the grid.[4]

Hence, this monumental edifice stands as the central foundation stone and cipher for the entire planetary consciousness.

Viewing this complex coded structure from a number of perspectives, a greater understanding of its higher functions comes forth. As a double pyramid, mirrored above ground and below ground, the Great Pyramid was constructed as a crucible in which the fusion of terrestrial energies with celestial Light would occur. This archetypal form is integrally associated with the element of fire, the alchemical element that instills the life-force. On this subject, Plato stated: "That solid which has taken the form of a pyramid shall be the element and seed of fire."[5] Indeed, the root meaning of *pyramid* is flame in the middle.[6] John Michell, a well-known spiritual scientist, expresses the essence of this geometrical configuration through a numerological-alchemical perspective:

The whole secret of prehistoric science is expressed in the following equation, which proves the meaning of the Great Pyramid with a clarity beyond words: $1080 + 666 = 1746$.[7]

The numerological equivalent of both the Great Pyramid and the Holy Ghost is 1080; 666 represents the Earth-Sun energies and the element of fire; 1746 is the number of alchemical fusion and the mustard seed of the New Testament parable. The whole equation, therefore, presents a mathematical picture of an interdimensional meeting ground in which the blending and uniting of the Heavens and the Earth takes place.

The mustard seed—1746—provides greater insight into the seed-crystals of wholeness that lie within the Great Pyramid. Jesus, in the parable of the mustard seed, says of the Kingdom of God:

It is like a grain of mustard seed, which, when sown upon the ground is the smallest of all the seeds on earth; yet when it is sown it grows up and becomes the greatest of all shrubs, and puts forth large branches, so that the birds of the air make nests in its shade.[8]

This seed, "planted" within the pyramid, is the seed-crystal of the alchemical fire of fusion that creates a state of union and wholeness. As such, it is a metaphorical "seed" that both carries the blueprint for growth patterns and is the catalyst for the culminating coalescence into wholeness; the Alpha blueprint blossoms forth through the Omega patterns of wholeness. Correspondingly, the Alpha and Omega of the Great Pyramid are located at the crystal chamber at the inverted apex and the (missing) crystal capstone of the upper apex.

The Great Pyramid demonstrates the laws behind the pure growth of life, and the seed or crystal was placed on its apex to distil the solar spark, the element of fire by which the terrestrial life essence is fertilised.[9]

The crystal apex of the inverted terrestrial pyramid represents the perfection of the earthly energies and the blueprint patterns for their manifestation; it is the grain of mustard seed that is sown in the Earth. The crystal capstone of the upper pyramid is the seed-crystal of the Whole-Light Synthesis of the celestial realms; it is the seed that ". . . grows up and becomes the greatest of all shrubs. . . ."

Just as the rainbow appears in the heavens as a sign of God's Love and Light to mankind, so does the crystal come forth from the earth to bring a message of Light from the past as a promise of Love for the future.[10]

The Alpha crystal "come(s) forth from the earth to bring a message of Light" to unite with the Omega crystal "as a promise of Love for the future."

The macrocosm of the Great Pyramid is reflected in the microcosm of the human bio-energetic pyramid. As stated above, pyramidal harmonics are the fundamental building blocks of manifestation as well as a primary key to biophysical and consciousness evolution. So it is that the human bio-energetic system interfaces with pyramidal geometry.

. . . [T]he vehicle of the Pyramid-Sphinx has been placed in the "middle of the Earth" as a living model of Man's destiny to indwell in a higher evolutionary body once he can center his solar and magnetic energy with the alignment of the pyramid. . . .[11]

One of the codes that illustrates this conception is the Egyptian hieroglyphic ✕✕✕, meaning "(human) self." The hieroglyphic form itself can be proportionally enlarged and superimposed within the pyramidal form, exhibiting significant correlations (see Figure 3). As a whole, it fits perfectly within this structure, its top loop molding snugly within the apex. In addition, the twin spiral lines cross exactly at the floor level of the Queen's Chamber and one of the outermost loops passes through the middle of the King's Cham-

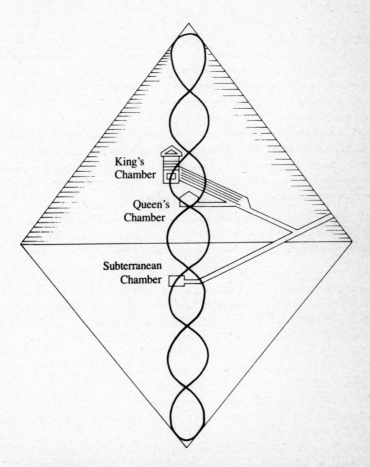

Figure 3: Egyptian Hieroglyph for "Self" in the Great Pyramid

ber at floor level.[12] Both of these chambers are considered to be primary energy accumulation areas. Further, consider the same "self" hieroglyphic mirrored in the inverted pyramid, producing a celestial "self" and the reflected image of an earthly "self," united at the midline between the two pyramids. This is representative of the ". . . cosmological pyramid of the Divine Overself coming into conjunction with the human biopyramid in the physical universe.[13]

Viewing the whole framework, then, we see a total of seven intersection areas formed by the double helix of the two united hieroglyphics—three above, three below, and one at the midline (formed by the union of the two "self" symbols). These seven areas correlate to the seven polarized chakras of the human bio-energetic system. Notably, several of the chambers within the anatomy of the Great Pyramid interrelate with these chakras. The sub-terranean chamber, or Chamber of Chaos, is located at the solar plexus area, and both the Queen's and King's Chambers are within the third-eye center. The heart chakra is situated at the intersection of the upper and lower pyramids, thus becoming the central point of fusion between the higher "self" and the lower "self." This region is also known as the Eye of Yahweh:

. . . [E]ach Pyramid of Light is energized by Yahweh's Eye in the center of the pyramid. This is the cosmological constant which enables every realm of intelligence to be reprogrammed into a higher level of creation.[14]

Also, J. J. Hurtak, in his book *The Book of Knowledge: The Keys of Enoch*, points to the Chamber of the Son as being a secret area that will ". . . open the hidden doors and unlock the final mysteries of the Pyramid."[15] According to the description of its location, it interfaces with the third-eye chakra along with the King's and Queen's Chambers. Note also that the correct proportions are left between the hieroglyphic double helix and the two apexes for the crystal capstones. Within the human bio-energetic pyramid, these two areas are the locations of the Alpha and Omega crystal chakras—the "seeds" of wholeness that encompass the seven chakras of dual polarity. Therefore, within the framework of what is known about the structure of the Great Pyramid, the human bio-energetic system synchronizes in significant ways that lead to further insight into the functioning of both complexes. Especially important is the depiction of the Alpha-Omega principle of wholeness that correlates to the crystal chakras that exist below the coccyx center and above the crown chakra. Thus the microcosmic human chakra system resonates with the macrocosmic evolutionary cycles—"beginning" in wholeness and "ending" in wholeness.

The integration of information concerning the octahedral geometry and the existence of the crystal apexes adds key information toward increased comprehension of the overall pyramidal energy dynamics (see Figure 4). Consider the Great Pyramid as it was originally constructed, with white (micro-crystalline) marble covering

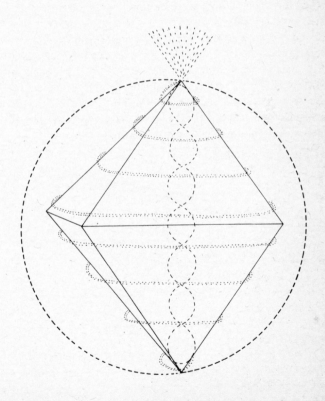

Figure 4: Pyramidal Energy Dynamics

the outer structure and the crystal capstones in place. The three major areas of energy generation and amplification are the Eye of Yahweh at the center of the octahedron and the two crystal capstones. While incoming energy enters and is transmitted from each one of these locations in complex ways, there is a *primary* energy pattern that encompasses the pyramid as a whole while the other more secondary energy dynamics takes place. Within this primary pattern, energy enters through the upper capstone, is amplified, and then sent downward around the exterior in spirals according to the mathematical ratio of *phi* (1:1.618 . . .). These spirals travel both clockwise and counterclockwise, expanding around the upper pyramid and then contracting along the lower pyramid until they unite at the lower crystal apex. Here these energies fuse intensely, are amplified and modulated, and then shoot upward very quickly in the manner of a laser beam. The seven pyramidal chakras are, in reality, standing waves (or fixed patterns) through which the energy moves. This Light-beam is again fused, amplified, and modulated in the upper capstone and then shot upward. The outgoing energy is also laserlike in nature—the main body of this Light-beam is propelled straight upwards very powerfully and the other secondary by-products curve around the outside of the pyramid in arcs, entering again at the lower crystal capstone for reintegration. Thus, it is within the framework of these overall energy dynamics that the other many complex Light-interactions take place.

By applying this knowledge of the primary energy pattern of the Great Pyramid to the human bio-energetic pyramid, a powerful modality of self-transformation arises. The basic idea is to use the principles of pyramidal energy dynamics that are already inherent within the human chakra system. In so doing, we activate the seeds of wholeness within ourselves and accelerate the rate of the harmonization and evolutionary progress of the entire bio-energetic system. These techniques can aid significantly in such holistic therapies as acupressure, massage, and chakra balancing, and in the myriad forms of meditation and spiritual self-transformation. The first step is to work with internal energies according to one's own chosen methods. The next step is to apply the pyramidal energy dynamics by *allowing* Light to be drawn into the Omega crystal-chakra (4–6 inches above the crown) and then feeling it spiral down around the body, expanding to the heart chakra and contracting down to the Alpha crystal chakra (4–6 inches below the coccyx). Here the energy is united, amplified, and propelled upward directly through the seven chakras, and then again going into the Omega chakra. After the Light is fused and amplified here, it is shot straight upward to infinity. One of the main keys in this method is to be as relaxed as possible and to allow the process to occur from a detached perspective. While this is in contradistinction to the various techniques of using willpower to force or direct energies from the lower to the higher chakras, it amplifies the *inherent* resonating pattern of energy dynamics within the human bio-energetic system. Therefore, it is in the mode of ''passive'' visualization of what is already existent that the best results will be received. Some will find that this procedure occurs in natural cycles of build up and release, build up and release, and so on; others will find that the process happens continuously. Also helpful is the placement of crystals, pointed upward, at both crystal chakras and any or all of the other seven centers. The last 5–10 minutes of a holistic therapy session or one's own period of inner work would be an optimal time to incorporate this technique. With regular practice, much dormant energy will be activated through this resonation with fundamental pyramidal harmonics.

An extended meditation using this conception is found in the ''Crystal Meditations'' chapter. A more basic meditation/visualization that can be done is as follows: When in a calm and relaxed physical and mental condition, visualize your whole chakra system from Alpha to Omega as existing within a pyramidal octahedron, the heart center being at the midline between the upper and lower pyramids. Visualize White Light being drawn from the cosmos through the Omega crystal chakra, concentrated, and then sent in both clockwise and counterclockwise spirals around the outside of the envisioned octahedron. Feel the expansion of the spiral currents to the heart chakra and then the gradual contraction down to the Alpha crystal chakra. Feel the energies being strongly fused and amplified, and then shot straight upward through all the chakras. Become one with this Light as it is amplified again in the

Omega capstone and shot like a laser beam to the higher celestial
realms. Ascend into the Light-body. Continue this cyclical sequence
until you feel as if you *are* a being of dazzling White Light.

. . . [T]he body of Man will go through the pyramid of flesh and crystal
and be transfigured into the next Pyramid of Light. . . .[16]

In summary, the seed-crystals of wholeness exist as capstones of
the negative and positive polarities of manifest creation. The archetypal Great Pyramid, as a fundamental keystone, embodies the
codes that catalyze the transmutation of the human bio-energetic
system into higher octaves of Light. Just as this Pyramid of Light
contains two crystal capstones of activation and wholeness, so does
the human chakra system have Alpha and Omega crystal chakras
that encompass the seven polarized energy centers. As our world
moves rapidly toward the Omega transition point, we are in the
midst of the greatest transformational sequence that the Earth has
experienced since its inception. As this occurs we are given the
means to make this evolutionary hero's journey through Light-based
healing techniques and technologies. Physics, metaphysics, and
holistic health alchemically unite through Divine Science to provide
the crystal pyramidal capstone toward ever-expanding Light-fields
of perfection. Let it be so.

Chapter 5

QUARTZ CRYSTALS

Tools of Healing and Self-Transformation

In essence, quartz crystals are tuning forks vibrating on multidimensional octaves of Light. Just as a tuning fork evokes a like-vibrational response from a receptive medium, so crystals facilitate an attunement with the harmonic vibrational tonalities of Light. These tools of Light resonate with the Light within each individual and thus assist in the process of evolutionary unfoldment. For this is their primary function—to evoke a like-response, a Light-response, in serving as interdimensional windows of Light.

It is crucially important to perceive and use crystals as *tools*— as a very helpful, though not necessary, means of self-transformation. Edgar Cayce has expressed this point very eloquently:

At these are but lights, but signs in thy experience, they are as but a candle that one stumbles not in the dark. But worship *not* the light of the candle; rather worship that to which it may guide thee in thy service. . . . . They only attune self so that Christ-consciousness may give the message! Listen to no message of a stone, of a number, even of a star; for they are but servants of the Lord and Master of all—even as thou.[1]

The crystal is not a message unto itself; it acts only as a tool through which the inner Light of one's own being is clarified. It is always of the utmost importance to look first and foremost to the wisdom of inner guidance, the "still, small voice within." In this way the quartz crystal helps to evoke greater attunement with the "inner crystal" that is our very own Higher Self.

In the evolutionary overview, crystals are a stepping-stone, an intermediate step, on the pathways to Divine realization. At the present point in the Earth's evolutionary sequence, crystals are a very potent and exceedingly helpful means of preparing for the next quantum growth phase into the fourth-dimensional Light-frequencies. Overall, though, they are tools that, having performed their function, can be put aside as marking stones on a pathway to the highest realms of Light. With greater perspective, we are less likely to blindly follow the messages of stones, numbers, planets, stars, and the like.

The crystals are bearers of great energy and shall serve you for as long as your need for them exists. In time you shall put them to the side, for they shall not be necessary for you to use. You shall only use them in a demonstration or in instructing someone else in their proper usage, until the time comes, when they too shall put them aside. This is evolution and we must evolve step by step, level by level, utilizing what is given us until we have reached the point where we may place these tools aside and stand along with our Father.[2]

Keeping these thoughts firmly in mind, let us explore the multifaceted applications of quartz crystals. Each of the following guidelines and ideas are presented more as seed-thoughts than as crystallized rules and unequivocal facts. Much knowledge has yet to be re-collected, and what is presented below can be creatively modified and expanded according to individual inner guidance. These tools can be used in a wide spectrum of ways, and it is for each individual to find that which is in accord with one's own highest spiritual needs and creative talents.

Crystal Categories

Each and every quartz crystal is basically composed of millions and millions of microscopic molecular spirals that form a highly ordered three-dimensional latticework that composes the entire crystal. This crystalline structure will respond in precise and predictable ways to the full spectrum of energies, including heat, light, pressure, sound, electricity, X-rays, gamma rays, microwaves, bio-electromagnetism, and thought-waves. In response to each type of energy, the molecules will oscillate back and forth at high speeds, thereby creating specific vibratory frequencies that unite together and pulse throughout the whole structure. These pulses are then transmitted from the crystal to the surrounding environment. The ways in which energy can be processed through the crystals are numerous and include the functions of reception, reflection, refraction, magnification, transduction, amplification, focusing, transmutation, transference, transformation, storage, capacitance, stabilization, modulation, balancing, and transmittance. Thus we can visualize the crystal as a vast network of spirals that receives energy, processes it along orderly pathways, and then transmits the collective oscillations outward in precise vibratory patterns.

Within this basic overview, there are many variations on the same theme. According to the different vibrational qualities that are infused into a particular crystal at the time of its formation or at various times thereafter, most crystals can be placed into categories of specialized functions. Each category has a characteristic manner of receiving, processing, and transmitting energy, therefore making each group more suitable for a specific kind of use. This is not to say that some overlapping of categories does not happen or that those of a particular grouping cannot perform other functions. Indeed, the majority of these tools have the capacity to serve a wide spectrum of purposes. However, many of them are *better* suited to operate in specific ways than others. And it is in using them as specialized tools that their highest potential is realized.

Let us take an overall view of these various categories in order to get an idea of the basic characteristics of each. In the rest of this chapter, factors concerning the practical applications of each of these groupings will be given at appropriate times.

1. *Power rods:* Crystals of exceptional inherent power that greatly amplify thought-forms and project them in a laserlike beam. These are power tools of the highest order, and the relatively few in existence generally gravitate to specific individuals. In one sense, they are tools of ''battle,'' for they can be used as swords of Light, cutting through apparent ''darkness'' with swiftness and efficiency. In another sense, the amplified thought-forms have a significant capability to initiate changes on the more causal levels of reality.

2. *Devic crystals:* As many shamans realized, certain factions of the devic kingdom use crystals as a ''home base''—a

focal point of grounding, recharging, rejuvenation, and interdimensional communication. It is best for these crystals not to be used as tools for human self-transformation, as they serve their function much better when maintained in a positive and relatively secluded environment.

3. *Attunement crystals:* A very general category that characteristically emanates highly charged, coherent Light-vibrations. They serve primarily as "tuning forks" of a particular frequency that can be used to help the attunement process in meditation, increase the vibrational quality of an environmental setting, or to "key" an individual's overall vibratory level to a specific harmonic of Light when worn or carried on a regular basis.

4. *Energy crystals:* A group that has been programmed to receive high intensities of interdimensional energies and, when activated, is a long-lasting source of energy output. Such crystals were used, for example, in Atlantis as energy generators that provided continual energy for a wide variety of purposes. Sometimes known as fire crystals, they have undergone a complex alchemical process whereby the DNA grid structure is directly attuned to higher-octave crystals of a similar nature. The intense Light from the higher dimensions bypasses many levels of modulatory processing through a complex series of interdimensional pathways, thus facilitating a relatively direct transference process.

5. *Healing crystals:* Tools that have a unified electromagnetic field that tends to evoke a like-response of harmony and balance. This energy field diffuses dullness, congestion, and imbalance, absorbs it, and reactivates innate perfection and wholeness. For this reason, it is quite important to regularly "clear" them of accumulated static energy (this process will be described later in this chapter). Within this broad category, different crystals operate with greater emphasis and efficiency on a particular level of functioning within the spirit-mind-emotions-body unity. That is, they all work to some degree with all levels, but many of them have areas of specialized capabilities.

6. *Energy rods:* Crystals that act primarily to attract, store, and periodically release energy. As they accumulate a ''charge,'' this energy can be infused by focused awareness into specific or general levels of the human aura. These ''cosmic batteries'' are used in a cyclical manner—allowing them to be charged, releasing the stored energy, and then charging again for further use.

7. *Archetype crystals:* A group that has been programmed by an aspect of the Universal Mind with a specific thought impression or thought sequence. The crystalline DNA structure has been activated in such a way as to store messages or codes to be received by specific individuals at appropriate points in time. The messages are usually of an informational nature, acting to reveal higher knowledge to those with the ''keys'' to activate and integrate such crystals.

8. *Library crystals:* These are similar to archetype crystals but have the capacity to receive and store greater amounts and wider degrees of information. It is like the difference between a single book and a set of encyclopedias. Tremendous amounts of knowledge are preserved in such crystals, awaiting the appropriate individuals to re-collect it at the right times. In addition, there are also many nonprogrammed library crystals that can be used today to store desired information.

9. *Numerological crystals:* Specifically coded tools that act to modify incoming Light-projections according to their very particularized programming. As crystals of a relatively fixed nature, their higher-octave use is a very technical matter. Currently, many of them function as transmission centers through which various Light-beings may send complex energy frequencies to the Earth-plane. They usually gravitate to definite persons, and it is generally only necessary to provide them with a positive environment without actively using them.

10. *Abominological crystals:* Those crystals that have acquired a distorted vibration through improper use. In general, quartz is able to be used with Light or spiritual ignorance according to the discrimination and intention of the one who uses it.

And at numerous intervals in history various crystals have been so misused, acquiring a tendency to misdirect energies into imbalanced patterns. Though this category is relatively uncommon, awareness of their existence is important, especially to those who work extensively with quartz. Only with very powerful Light-rays can they be cleared of distorted programming. The best course of action is usually to bury them underground in a remote area and ask higher Light-beings to take care of them appropriately.

11. *Transmitting crystals:* A group that transmits Light-projections with clarity and integrity. These are excellent tools to amplify and project thought-forms from one location to another. Crystals of this type usually have a wide spectrum of modification potential; that is, they are able to process many degrees and varieties of the Light-spectrum.

12. *Modulatory crystals:* A very broad and general category whose primary function is to receive and modify incoming Light within relatively wide parameters. Closely akin to numerological crystals, the modulatory type serves a much larger range of functions and is not as tightly programmed. Like the healing crystals, specific modulatory tools are better able to perform certain more specialized roles than others, but all have generalized capacities within the whole spectrum of Light-interactions.

13. *Vision crystals:* Those crystals that increase the abilities of inner "sight" associated with the third-eye area. Specifically attuned to the frequencies of the third-eye chakra, this group acts to amplify and clarify this vibratory level. They can analogously be viewed as binoculars that serve to extend and fine-tune inner vision into higher octaves of functioning.

14. *Toning, or "singing," crystals:* A subcategory of attunement crystals, having a more specific, less variable energy frequency. They are similar to the numerological category in the relative fixity of programming. As specialized "tuning forks," they are best used by certain individuals in particular circumstances. As a set of such tools used in different sequences and combinations, they are very effective healing and attuning agents.

15. *Surgery crystals:* Crystals programmed to be used for "psychic surgery" and very precise alterations of auric energy patterns. The vibrational intensity of this group is very high and set in exact grid patterns that facilitate the axial parting of the physical body or the energy "bodies" according to the thought projections of the operator. This phenomenon can also be called crystal white-Light surgery.

16. *Open-ended, or generalized, crystals:* A very broad group with generalized capacities to be programmed for any number of purposes according to intention. They can be viewed as blank cassette tapes, ready to serve in a wide spectrum of uses. Again, crystals in this category may *tend* to lend themselves more to various functions but can be effective through a wide range.

Clearly, then, quartz crystals can be categorized as distinct tools that perform myriad functions according to their inherent programming. The instrument of quartz is that aspect of creation that imbues the qualities of order and precision within the multifaceted expressions of Light. To know the optimal use of particular crystals is to be able to employ them for what they truly are—specialized tools used for Light, by Light, and in Light.

Introductory Crystal Awareness

Working with crystals is a process of continuing discovery and deepening awareness of the crystalline nature of all manifest creation. As this occurs, the crystal becomes less and less a mere physical object of beauty and more and more a living medium of dynamic precision and wholeness. Look at the crystal before you and see a reflection of your own higher nature. As windows of Light, they serve as an extension of the self into harmonic octaves of Light, leading toward a realization of "self" as pure crystalline Light.

Let us begin this journey of discovery with some introductory awareness exercises that will start the process of sensing the inner life of these apparently inert objects. Presented below is a sequence of such exercises that can be done singly or, optimally, in succession.

In each one, take plenty of time to notice the subtle energy changes and interactions that occur. Observe them passively and with full concentration. Blend your energies with those of the crystal, and start to see it for what it truly is—Light!

1. In a relaxed and clear frame of mind, pick up a crystal and hold it comfortably in your left hand. Close your eyes and calmly focus inward, paying close attention to any sensations and perceptions that arise over a period of 2–5 minutes.

2. Next, repeat the same process, but this time hold the crystal for 30–45 seconds and then place it away from yourself for the same amount of time. Go through several cycles of this procedure, noticing the change(s).

3. Now rub the thumb of your left hand back and forth on one of the larger facets on the top of the crystal. Repeat this motion for 15–30 seconds and then simply hold it still for the same length of time. Go through several cycles of this process.

4. For this next exercise, roll the crystal between both hands for 15–30 seconds and then hold it still in your left hand for 30–45 seconds. Repeat this several times.

5. Now roll the crystal between the hands again for 30 seconds and then place it on the heart chakra or third-eye center for 30–45 seconds. Repeat several cycles of this exercise.

6. Take 5–10 minutes to look at the crystal from as many angles and perspectives as possible. Alternately close your eyes and try to reconstruct in your mind's eye the three-dimensional image that was viewed from a particular angle. Many people find that this is one of the best ways to get to "know" a crystal.

7. Next, rotate the crystal in front of each chakra for 30–45 seconds and then hold it still in this position for 15–20 seconds. Start from the lower chakras and work upward.

8. For the final introductory exercise, hold the crystal directly in front of the third-eye center. Focus your awareness at the third eye and send thought energy directly into the crystal. Do this in a concentrated way for 30 seconds and then relax the concentration while still retaining a passive awareness of the crystal. Repeat this for several cycles.

Use the crystal meditations in Chapter 6 for more advanced awareness exercises. It is very helpful to place these meditations on cassette tape in order to be able to relax into the process more readily and for repeated use.

There are many other exercises that can be done for cultivating a deeper rapport with the crystal kingdom, limited only by one's creativity and curiosity. So use the above guidelines as a starting point for further exploration, and as this chapter proceeds many other possibilities will also be introduced.

Choosing a Crystal

The choosing of a personal crystal is a very individual matter, best done with sensitivity to crystal energies and one's own inner wisdom. The basic goal is to find a crystal (or crystals) that resonates with your own unique vibratory patterns. Each crystal is also unique in its energy frequencies, and it is best to find the crystal that blends most harmoniously with you. For one crystal may catalyze much growth in one person while it may do little for another. Sometimes, a crystal will magnetically attract attention immediately—there is an instant rapport that leaves no doubt that it is to be "your" personal tool. Other times, in passing your hands over a group of crystals, you will feel especially strong energies from a few or your eyes may keep coming back to certain ones. Pick up those for which you feel attraction and feel the energies through your hands. Look at the details—the clarity, angles, mirrors, rainbow reflections, and so on. Establish a rapport with it. If necessary, do a few awareness exercises with it, like those described in the preceding section. For those who employ pendulums, this can also be a useful method of selection. Eventually, as you come into contact with the appropriate crystal(s) for personal use, there will be an inner awareness that signals that it is the right one for you.

Clearing and Cleansing

Within the molecular latticework, various forms of negative or static energies tend to accumulate over a period of time due to its sensitivity to energetic influences. These influences include electronic pollution, negative thought-forms, absorption of imbalances in healing work, and negative emotions. Each crystal has various auric energy levels, just as the human auric system. Basically, the primary programming—the core level—retains its integrity in spite of disharmonious energies. It is the more secondary auric levels that are relatively sensitive to the energetic environment, and as static energies accumulate on these levels the functioning of the whole crystal will be reduced. Overall, the strength of a crystal's aura will repel a significant percentage of surrounding imbalanced energies but will still process some of these influences, again exactly as the human auric system does. It is the energies that are strong and/or are relatively constant that affect crystals the most. In particular, they are sensitive to strong emotions and thoughts, and therefore it is important to keep them away from oneself when experiencing negativity—anger, grief, sadness, and so on. In addition to retaining the residues of these energies, they will also reflect these imbalances back into the auric environment, thus intensifying them. Whenever a crystal has been exposed to these types of situations, it is well to cleanse it. Also, when a crystal is first received and when it has been used for healing work, it is a good practice to cleanse it shortly thereafter. In general, too, it is optimal to put all crystals through such a maintenance ritual once every two weeks. Those that are worn or carried regularly should go through this process once a week. Quartz is continuously exposed to myriad forms of energy, and the practice of clearing and cleansing keeps the latticework at its highest level of functioning.

These are many ways in which the process of *clearing* can be done. Listed below are several of these methods—all work well either singly or in combination. Experiment with these procedures and find those that work best for you.

1. Pack in salt for 24–48 hours.
2. Bury underground for 2–7 days.
3. Place in running water—streams, rivers, and so on—for 5–7 days.
4. Place in salt water for 24–48 hours.
5. Pack in clay for 3–5 days.

These methods will facilitate a thorough clearing of static "debris." For a quick clearing in between the more thorough processes, a couple of methods work well:

1. Hold the crystal under cold, running water between both hands for 30–60 seconds, visualizing bright white Light going through the crystal.
2. Hold the crystal in both hands and take in a slow, deep breath. Hold the breath for a few seconds while focusing on the crystal. Exhale quickly in a burst, visualizing and feeling all static energy being released from the latticework. Repeat this process several times.

The *cleansing* of crystals is a very simple procedure used to clean away any remaining "loose" static energies. After using one or more of the above methods for clearing, place the crystal in cold, running water for approximately 30 seconds. As this is done, visualize white Light surrounding and penetrating the quartz. Afterwards, it is ready for use once again.

Clearing and cleansing are very important, for without them crystals tend to become more and more dulled and ineffective. Through taking the time and effort to care for these tools with the methods just outlined, the clarity and "sparkle" will be maintained in them, and you.

Charging and Activating

Once a crystal has been cleared and cleansed of static residue, the next step is to recharge the molecular latticework with positive energies. The basic principle is to place the quartz in an environment that infuses it with energy frequencies that "prime" it for use. This is a twofold process—charging involves the building up of an energy charge (like a battery) and activating concerns the catalyzing of dormant areas of the crystal's energy spectrum. In most all quartz the full range of the potential energy dynamics is not fully operational and therefore needs certain stimuli to activate its optimal functioning. There are many methods for accomplishing charging and activation, and it is worthwhile to try a number of them to see which one(s) suits you and your crystal(s) best.

These methods include:

1. Place the crystal in direct outdoor sunlight and moonlight for 24–48 hours. This is a very effective procedure and the most popularly used.
2. Snowstorms, rainstorms, and other dynamic weather conditions are especially useful for activation purposes.
3. Set the crystal inside a pyramid at a general location or a specific energy area, such as the King's Chamber, Queen's Chamber, and apex. This will charge the quartz with pyramid energy.
4. Extremes of heat and cold aid in activating a wider range of energy frequencies.
5. Put the crystal-tool at a "power spot," such as a mountaintop, holy place, or energy vortex, for both charging and activation.
6. Exposing quartz to a wide spectrum of colors is helpful for activation. This can be done either by shining colors through a slide projector or placing color gels or colored glass on top of the crystal in direct sunlight and moonlight.
7. Create a circle of crystals, pointing inward to the middle, and place the crystal to be charged in the center. This is best done in direct outdoor light for 24–48 hours.
8. Set a crystal outside in a relatively remote location and communicate with higher-dimensional Light-beings of your choice, asking them to assist in the charging and activation process.

Once completed, it is a good idea to recharge crystals after every cycle of clearing and cleansing. Be creative in trying new ideas and combinations of various methods. Experimentation and experience are your best teachers.

Wearing and Carrying Crystals

The wearing or carrying of a personal crystal can serve to stabilize and balance the whole auric system. Quartz is very responsive to the bio-electromagnetism and other energy spectrums of the human aura, and by keeping a selected crystal in close proximity for a period of 2–4 weeks. it becomes attuned to the unique energy patterns of the individual. The programming of the crystal becomes "keyed" to one's personal vibrations, and it then becomes a reflection and extension of oneself. Just as the crystal-plates in electronic oscillators keep an energy frequency steady, so the quartz crystal aids in stabilizing the energy dynamics of the entire aura. One result is that the various ups and downs of spiritual, mental, emotional, and biological cycles will tend to be evened out towards a greater overall balance. In addition, the personal crystal processes the auric energies through its structure, absorbs imbalanced energy fluctuations, and then sends back these energies in a more balanced format. Therefore, the total auric system is held steady at an optimal frequency level. This whole process also makes it more difficult for disease patterns to take hold due to the increased stability and balance of overall vibrations. On another level, the crystal tends to protect the individual from incoming negative influences by taking them into the crystalline structure before they are processed through the person's aura. There are many reports of small cracks or implosions appearing in personal crystals that have not been physically dropped or knocked. This is usually an indication that it has absorbed and held some form of potentially harmful energy. Additionally, these tools function as a "window" through which higher-dimensional Light-beings can project energies that will be held steady within the crystal and passed on to the individual for purposes of healing and self-transformation. Thus, personal crystals become an extension of the self in which energy patterns can be positively processed and stabilized.

The process of programming a crystal to be a personal tool is an important one. First, the right crystal must be selected, cleared, cleansed, charged, and activated, as discussed earlier in this chapter. The crystal categories commonly used in this capacity are toning (14), modulatory (12), and attunement (3) crystals. (The number in parentheses following the name of the category refers to the number of the explanatory paragraph found earlier in this chapter.) Next, the tool should be kept within the personal aura for a period of 2–4 weeks. This can be done by carrying it in the pockets or purse, or wearing it as a pendant. At night, it can be kept in a pillowcase or somewhere else in close proximity. It is very beneficial during this time to do a brief clearing and cleansing each day. Performing a number of awareness and meditation exercises with the crystal will also facilitate the deepening of the mutual blending of energies. Keep in mind that the quartz is becoming an extension of yourself and that whatever affects it will affect you. Try as much as possible to keep it away from any negative influences or direct contact with other peoples' vibrations—the time of initial programming is a sensitive stage. This whole process can be a very enriching one as you make the crystal a friend, companion, and co-worker.

One of the most popular and practical ways of wearing a personal crystal is as a pendant located over the heart chakra. This energy center is the area where many external influences are first received and is also the seat of the life-force. On the physical level, it is the location of the thymus gland, one of the body's major areas of stress reactivity. A pendant worn here will act as a personal crystal as well as strengthening the heart-chakra functions. Generally speaking, it is preferable that the pendant not be capped as well as left in its natural state unless it is precisely and purposely faceted for one's own being. A pendant with the crystal pointed downward will produce a soothing, calming, and energizing effect on the body; with the point going upward, the spirit is strengthened and uplifted; and a doubly terminated crystal performs both processes.

Two of the most common and convenient ways of carrying a personal crystal are in the front pants pocket or in a purse. With these modes of carrying quartz, it is especially important to protect them from damage sustained from other objects in the pockets or purse. Even though crystals are very hard minerals, they can still be chipped and abraded when bumped into other objects. By placing them in a pouch or wrapping them in a soft protective covering, they will be better able to maintain their highest integrity and beauty. Many have found that natural fiber materials such as silk and cotton serve this purpose best.

Programming Crystals

All through the ages wise men have known that crystal is a most powerful memory bank. It vibrates with electric pulses. In it every thought is imprinted, recorded and stored. Of all the substances on Earth, it is the most like living matter. . . . Crystal is the only material on Earth which holds this knowledge. To enter is to know.[3]

Crystals are in actuality computer devices that process information according to the structure of the molecular spiral latticework in conjunction with the DNA programming of each individual molecular unit. As described in Chapter 3, the element of silicon is the primary basis for the computer memory and programming. It is the ability of silicon to store and release electrical charges with great precision and order that makes it such an important part of computer technology. Quartz crystals operate similarly, though their main differences are that quartz is an "intelligent" medium and is able to interact very responsively with thought-waves. In Chapter 2, it was seen that crystals are an order of Intelligence—a sentient level of consciousness evolving according to its own chosen patterns. The "mind" of crystals is similar to the human mind in terms of their holographic and electromagnetic manner of functioning. Essentially, mind *is* order; and so it is that the human mind can effectively program the internal dynamics of the crystal mind. The interaction is one of thought-forms projected into the internal crystalline matrix and the holding of the pattern of these thoughts steady until they are sufficiently impressed within the crystal. The nature of the "thoughts" that can be programmed are multitudinous—they can be specific images or information, channeled energies (e.g., healing energy, higher knowledge), sound, color, geometric patterns, specific energy frequencies, and so on. The key in this whole process is *intention*—it is this keynote that forms the "latticework" of the programming. This is to say that spiritual awareness and feeling are more important than conscious knowledge, and it is in extending the conscious mind into the higher octaves of the Universal Mind that the highest programming of crystals will be done. In this way, it is Divine Intelligence channeled through the human mind that does the programming. This is why crystals in particular are the quintessential medium for this process, for they are "windows of Light" that set into motion amplified and clarified spiritual-mental energies into the higher octaves of Light.

Effective crystal programming necessitates precise control of thought-forms, both in visualizing an image clearly in the mind's eye and in holding this image steady and projecting it into the crystal. This is a skill that may take some time and practice in developing, but is well worth the effort because of the mental control and holographic imaging capabilities that will evolve to greater degrees. Toward this end, there are a number of exercises that can be practiced that will facilitate increasing effectiveness in crystal programming. Take plenty of time with each aspect of the exercises presented below—enjoy the process of self-discovery.

1. Focus awareness on the third-eye area and feel the energy progressively accumulating. Hold a crystal out in front of the third eye and practice projecting this energy into the quartz-tool. Experiment with holding the crystal at different distances and at various angles, noticing the accompanying changes as the energy feeds back to your consciousness.

   Practice visualizing your thought-energy being projected in a laserlike beam. Experiment with holding the crystal at various distances and angles, trying to find the point of optimal energy exchange between you and the crystal. Keep fine-tuning these laser thought-waves in relationship to the quartz.

2. An excellent exercise to do at this point is the "Sensing the Crystal Meditation" presented in Chapter 7, "Crystal Meditations." This will increase awareness of the internal sensations and structure of the crystalline latticework and prepares the way for further exercises.

3. Proficiency in holographic visualization is very helpful in crystal programming. One exercise to increase this ability involves looking at a crystal from numerous angles and perspectives. Try to notice all the three-dimensional details from a particular perspective and then close your eyes and reconstruct it in your mind's eye. Stay with this perspective until you can visualize it fully—the angles, internal shapes and forms, clarity, and so on. If necessary, open your eyes to get a better picture and then close them again, reconstructing it once more. Five to ten minutes of this procedure done every day or so for two weeks will bring noticeable improvements in holographic imaging abilities. This exercise has also been found to be helpful in developing a better memory.[4]

4. Now, with a crystal held in front of the third eye, create a holographic image, preferably of a higher nature. See it as vividly as possible and hold it steady within the mind. Next,

project it into the latticework, following the image with your awareness as you, too, enter the crystalline matrix. Center your awareness within this structure and concentrate on holding the image steady. Observe how it interacts with the latticework of the crystal. Keep holding the image until you feel that it has been imprinted sufficiently within the quartz so that it will remain.

Repeat this same process several times with different images. Before working with another image, though, go back into the crystal and visualize the image that is already there dissipating and leaving the structure. Some people find that this "erasing" procedure is helped by taking in a breath, holding it, and expelling it quickly. During the exhalation, see the image also being expelled from the crystal.

If you have a partner to work with, try implanting an image, and then giving the crystal to the other person to see if he or she can perceive the image accurately.

Another aspect of crystal programming involves the use of pure intention—projected energy without an image-form. For example, if another person asks for healing work to be done, the crystal can be used as a receptive medium for healing energy channeled from Divine Intelligence. In this mode of programming, again, it is the blending of the human mind with Universal Mind that facilitates the best results. This aspect of channeling "intention" can be used in myriad ways, limited only by one's creativity.

The importance of this aspect of crystal programming lies in its emphasis on clearly formulating one's intention with as much precision as possible. Then, when this formulated intention is connected with higher octaves of Divine Intelligence, the clarity and strength of the vibrations channeled into the crystal are much greater. Crystalline intention imprinted within a crystal charges and amplifies its level of functioning to a much higher degree.

It is the authors' viewpoint that each individual has the innate wisdom and ability to apply crystal energies in ways that suit the person's own unique spiritual needs and talents. Toward this end, the suggestions presented below (and all others) offer general principles and guidelines for experimentation and self-application.

1. In an attunement crystal (3)—a tool of a very precise vibration—the channeling of higher-octave harmonic energies can serve to activate a greater portion of the crystal's total energy spectrum and amplify the intensity of its emanations.

2. In a modulatory crystal (12)—one that modifies energy according to a relatively broad programming—the latticework can be transformed into a more precise pattern that would more efficiently serve a particular purpose.

3. With a healing crystal (5), the programming can be modified to resonate with the energies of specific chakras, body systems, emotional dynamics, and so on. This is to say that a healing tool with an inherent ability to work with a distinct level of healing can be made into an even more precise and efficient instrument.

4. With an energy rod (6)—a crystal "battery" that accumulates and discharges energy—patterns and frequencies of vibrations that may be needed at a particular point in time can be channeled from Divine Intelligence into the crystal and then discharged appropriately.

5. In the realm of self-transformation, a vibration or energy pattern that is needed at a particular period of time to facilitate this process can be programmed and held steady using such crystal categories as attunement (3), vision (13), healing (5), modulatory (12), archetype (7), and toning (14), as appropriate to one's needs.

6. A devic crystal (2) can be better prepared for its utilization as a "home" for aspects of the devic kingdom through charging and activating the inherent programming in conjunction with Divine Intelligence.

There are many other ways to use this principle of applying unified spiritual intention into a crystal in order to modify and/or activate its programming for further use. Experiment with different approaches and applications that blend with your own inner awareness and unique spiritual needs.

Another programming method involves the transference of focused intention through the hands into the quartz. The hands can be employed as sensitive transmitters of thought-waves, both in image-form and in pure energy frequencies. Hold a crystal between both hands, establish rapport with it, and open the awareness to higher-dimensional Light. Form the intent and focus it strongly within the mind. Hold the image or energy frequency steady until there is a natural impetus towards transferring the programming. Allow the energies to be concentrated and focused through the hands, feeling the oscillations going back and forth between the hands and through the crystal. Gradually focus the energies into the crystalline matrix itself, visualizing the program holding steady within the latticework. Continue until it is sufficiently imprinted within the crystal. It is then a specialized tool to be used for its specified and desired purposes.

Not only can crystals retain programs that manifest through the channeling of spiritual intent but also can be infused with the energy-mechanics of such phenomenon as magnetism, pyramid energy, color, sound, and aromas. The basic difference in this mode of programming is the relatively linear nature of the encoding process. In this mode, a crystal is exposed to a distinct and coherent external influence for the purpose of holding the specific energy pattern within the crystalline matrix. For example, a quartz exposed exclusively to the color blue for a significant period of time will then be programmed to be a tool in which the quality and radiation pattern of blue will be the predominant influence. This is not to say that color frequencies emanating from the quartz will be exclusively blue, for all the colors will be present to a degree, but the *keynote* of that crystal will be blue. The same principle applies for magnetism, sound, pyramid energy, and so on—the holistic nature of quartz is not canceled but is *oriented* within a specific keynote energy pattern. The crystal is then a very specialized tool that can be applied in particular circumstances when that predominating frequency is appropriate. The optimal way of using these tools is, again, in connection with higher wisdom. For example, an individual may have numerous crystals of this nature, programmed as red, G flat, south magnetic pole, and so on; in order to accomplish a particular purpose, it would be best to attune to Divine Intelligence first and receive input as to the optimal manner and sequence of applying the tools at hand. In this way, spiritual wisdom is blended with "mechanical" tools.

This mode of programming is somewhat different from those discussed beforehand. They are similar, however, in terms of the initial establishment of rapport with the crystal and a connection with higher octaves of Light. Then, in place of channeling super-conscious energies and images, it is *primarily* the conscious mind that formulates and projects the basic intent. This does not mean that there is no blending of energies with the Universal Mind; rather, it is a difference of degree. Before applying the external vibration (i.e., color, sound, and so on), it is very helpful to prepare the quartz-tool by first projecting the idea of this influence into the latticework. For example, if a crystal is to be infused with the color violet, this process will be facilitated by mentally implanting the thought, visual image, and feeling of violet into the crystal. After this, place it in a relatively isolated location along with the vibration to be encoded. Try to keep any other external influences to a minimum during this sensitive stage. Experiment with the amount of time required to sufficiently program a crystal with various types of vibrations. Also, it is usually beneficial to re-energize the initial programming at various intervals as needed in order to keep the coding coherent and potent.

The potential applications in this realm of programming are limitless. Presented below are a sampling of these possibilities. Again, they are given only as principles and guidelines to work with as they apply to one's own unique spiritual needs and talents, guided by inner wisdom.

1. Colors, both singly and in combinations, are one of the easiest and most popular types of vibrations to program. There are two main methods: slide projector and translucent-colored materials of gel, plastic, or glass. With the slide projector, shine the color(s) into a crystal for 1–1½ hours per color. When the colored gel, plastic, or glass is used, place the quartz in direct sunlight and moonlight for 24–48 hours with the colored material positioned over as much of the crystal's surface as possible. If the material cannot cover the whole quartz, place it over the top facets for optimal results. During this process, rotate the crystal onto each side to expose the latticework to the color from different angles.

Some examples of how color programming can be applied include:

If the third-eye center needs the colors orange and violet to be emphasized, a vision crystal can be so modified.

A chakra needing blue, red, and green would be helped by a healing crystal with this coding.

If an inflamed kidney needs blue, an energy rod can be charged with this color and then infused into the kidney area.

A transmitting crystal may require certain color frequencies to be emphasized in order to better match its overall vibrations with those of the operator.

2. Single tones or specific musical chords can be encoded. Musical instruments of many varieties can be employed for this purpose. Simply play a tone or chord with the quartz in close proximity for 15–30 minutes. With different instruments there will be varying tonalities and timbre, therefore creating slightly varying effects in any one musical note or chord. Experiment with these variations.

The Spirit of Light produces vibratory divisions which, when audible are termed sound, or music, and when visible are named "colours or hues."[5]

Sound and color, then, are two aspects of the same fundamental energy. Therefore, sound can be used in the same basic ways as color, and the above examples given for color also apply to sound. In addition, programming color-sound combinations can also be used along these same lines.

3. Musical sequences and the ambient tones of Nature are other applications of sound. Whole symphonies, songs, and chants can be programmed into a crystal. For this, simply place the quartz in front or on top of the speaker system and play the piece of music in its entirety 3 times. Similarly, quartz can be programmed by one's voice, singing or intoning the desired sounds for 15–30 minutes. The sounds of Nature, on the other hand, can be encoded by placing the crystal in a relatively isolated location near the source of the vibration that is wanted, e.g., waterfall, trees blowing in the wind, river sounds, the stillness of the deep woods. Leave it at this location for 1–2

weeks. Thereafter, these "music crystals" can be placed in a meditation or sleeping area, used for emotional, mental, or spiritual balancing, and other creative uses according to one's intentions.

4. Exposing a crystal to either the north or south pole of a magnet will program these specific vibrations. In such books as *Magnetism and Its Effects on the Living System* by Albert Roy Davis and Walter Rawls, it has been found that each magnet pole has a multitude of healing applications. In general, the north pole has negative, soothing, and diminishing properties; the south pole has positive, strengthening, and expanding properties. This is an area with much experimentation potential.

5. Pyramids have proven to be energy accumulators and transmuters. Crystals placed in this environment can be charged and programmed with this amplified energy. Once coded in this manner, quartz will have many of the characteristics of pyramid energy. From food dehydration and preservation to spiritual upliftment and attunement, there are myriad uses of pyramids described in a number of good books.[6] Crystals programmed with pyramid energy can be used in corresponding ways.

6. Placing a crystal in a concentrated aromatic environment will encode this vibration. The spiritual and healing applications of aromatherapy will benefit from using quartz as a vibrational repository, transmuter, and transmitter. Chakras, for example, in need of a specific aromatic quality will receive this frequency more effectively with a programmed crystal placed on top of the energy center. In spiritual attunement, an individual may fine-tune deeper awareness through employing a crystal "tuning fork" of a specific fragrance. There are many other creative uses that can also be explored.

7. The qualities of particular weather conditions can be coded into a crystal-tool. Snowstorms, thunderstorms, soft rains, and so on can be programmed simply by placing a quartz in the midst of the weather phenomenon. Such crystals can be used in spiritual attunement, environmental harmonizing,

healing, and other functions in accordance with inner wisdom and creativity.

8. In the field of radionics, a specific radiational frequency or pattern can be programmed into quartz by irradiating it for 15–30 minutes (in general). The crystal can then be used by an individual as a continual emitter of this vibration and as an excellent receiving point for further transmissions from radionic devices.

9. The vibrational qualities of key vortex areas, holy places, and other "power spots" can be held within a crystal that is left at such a location for 3–7 days. These tools then also serve to maintain a more direct energetic link with that area.

Once a crystal has been programmed, it processes incoming energies in accordance with this program and continuously sends these specialized signals into the surrounding environment. In effect, it is a transmitting mechanism that steadily broadcasts its patterned messages. The strength of the transmissions depends upon the amount of energy that is processed through the crystal. In this regard, there is a baseline signal that is repeatedly disseminated when a quartz-tool is not consciously being used. This signal can still be significant in its effects in conjunction with auric energies and the subconscious mind. A healing crystal, for example, will facilitate the deep implantation of the healing pattern into the aura when it is used with focused awareness. Thereafter, whenever the crystal is in contact with the aura and subconscious mind while the conscious awareness is directed elsewhere (sleeping, working, and so on), it will continue to transmit the healing energies, though on a less intense energy level. Thus it will help to reinforce the healing process on the subliminal levels. When this tool is not within the auric field, it will continue to transmit the programmed signals, but these will be weak and relatively ineffective unless radionic principles are applied (to be discussed later in this chapter). Therefore, we see crystal-tools as perpetual transmission centers of their respective programming, the strength of which is directly proportional to the amount of incoming energies.

Multiple programs can also be encoded within a single crystal.

This process, known as multiplexing, is analogous to the 8-track cassette tapes that have several distinct and parallel channels. Similarly, a crystal is able to incorporate into its energetic latticework numerous programs that can operate distinctly and simultaneously. The process of multiplexing is basically identical to the single-programming procedures, except that the same crystal is used as another pattern is encoded. All the program levels operate simultaneously, though with applied awareness a single one can be activated to a greater degree and then applied appropriately. The multiple programs will interact with one another as the various energy patterns resonate throughout the crystalline structure. For this reason, it is more effective to create programs that are of a similar nature. In this way, each one is distinct and also reinforces the functioning of all the others. It is also important for both single and multiple codings to resonate with the nature of a particular crystal; that is, a vision crystal (for example) will not accommodate a healing program very effectively. Some quartz-tools operate optimally with only a single program while others work best with more. This must be discerned on an individual crystal-by-crystal basis. Thus the possibility of multiplexing adds a new dimension to be explored in the world of crystal "computers."

Once a particular program is no longer desired, it can be erased and replaced with another. This is a relatively simple procedure that dissolves an existing program and leaves the crystal open for restructuring. It is analogous to erasing a cassette tape, leaving it blank, and then recording new material in its place. In order to do this, first form the intent to erase and then project it into the quartz, holding it steady until the process is felt to be complete. In multiplexed crystals, separate programs can be erased and replaced while leaving the others intact. It is helpful in all cases to clear, cleanse, and charge the "erased" crystal and then proceed to reprogram it.

Advanced Programming Exercises

Presented below are a series of exercises designed to initiate increased understanding of the nature of the crystalline matrix and the thought-wave interactions within this matrix. Basic levels of proficiency in crystal programming skills are assumed; therefore the advanced techniques are given directly. Regular practice of these techniques will afford optimal results. Be open to new ideas and ways of relating to "thoughts" and "knowledge," for they are often of a different nature in the higher realms of Light!

1. Practice projecting thought-energy into a crystal. Find your own personal way of transmitting this laserlike energy in the most focused manner.

   Experiment with holding the crystal at different angles in relationship to the thought-energy. Each crystal has a somewhat unique way of receiving and processing thoughts.

   Visualize a laser beam of energy going from the third eye into the crystal. Feel how it interacts with the spiral molecular latticework. Follow this energy inside the crystal until you, too, are within its structure. Explore this new world of spirals, grids, lattices, angles, electricity, colors, and sounds.

   Expand your awareness until it fills the entire crystal. Notice how the quartz functions as a whole unit. Perhaps you will see how it operates holographically. Perceive how the angles of the facets interact with the energy flow.

   Go deeply within the quartz structure, and watch as interdimensional "windows" open before your awareness. Go through them feeling how the energy pulses between dimensions, connecting them, blending into one another in harmonic octaves of color and sound.

   Go from octave to octave, dimension to dimension, in sequential shifts of being. Practice this until you can do it smoothly and efficiently.

   Shift back to the physical-octave crystal, and slowly transfer awareness back to the body.

2. Once again, practice projecting a laser beam of thought-energy into a crystal at varying angles and intensities. Feel the changes in the flow of energy as it feeds back to your own consciousness.

   Project your awareness inside the crystalline matrix. This time, notice the nature of the colors and sounds as they course through the crystalline structure, intersecting and interplaying in a complex webwork of Light-interactions.

   Allow your consciousness to encompass the whole crystal

now, and feel the entire three-dimensional network of color-sound dynamics within your whole being.

Now introduce "thoughts" of color into the crystal. Try different colors and various color patterns. Watch as they go from level to level within the latticework. Notice how they interact with the already-existing patterns.

Introduce "thoughts" of sound into the crystal. Project different tone and tone patterns. Notice how they alter and intersect with the existing color-sound patterns.

Now "think" more complex sound *and* color patterns at once. Don't limit yourself—open up to new possibilities as you allow the Universal Mind to channel through your own being. Watch as the exquisitely precise and complex beauty of Divine Intelligence works within you. Notice the computerlike orderliness and complexity and at the same time the "play" and joy inherent in this process. Continue with this until you desire to shift back to physical awareness.

3. Now that there is sufficient experience in projecting into a crystal, simply do it with an easy economy of effort.

Once inside, become aware of the resonating octaves of Light that lie just beyond the crystal's interdimensional "window." Connect your consciousness with these reverberating octaves, feeling all the harmonic tonalities at once.

Watch as an image comes into your mind—see it clearly. Now allow Divine Intelligence to convert this image into a holographic color-sound pattern. Notice how this pattern relates to the crystal's latticework. Hold it for a comfortable period of time and then continue this same process with numerous other images that come to mind.

Next, reverse the procedure—allow a holographic color-sound pattern to come into your mind and then convert it into an image. Do this several times, watching the relationship between the images and the spiral molecular matrix.

4. Project your awareness into the crystal.

Feel your connection with the higher octaves of Light.

Practice for a few minutes the basic lessons of the preceding exercise—converting images into color-sound patterns, and vice versa.

Now for a more advanced application of these basic principles: Watch as a series of images flows through your mind. As each image in the sequence manifests, it instantaneously changes into a color-sound holograph. The whole series of images proceeds through a complex juxtaposition of the two modalities of perception, oscillating back and forth between an image and its corresponding color-sound grid.

The same principle can be reversed, converting a series of color-sound holographs into corresponding, parallel sequences of images.

This exercise in particular may take many practice sessions in order to gain proficiency with this mode of superconscious thinking. Continue with determination, for its applications in certain forms of higher-octave Light-work will become obvious in time.

Advanced Programming Applications

We are all crystals dissolved into light. Anything we wish to be, we are.[7]

The more advanced applications of crystal programming principles given below are seeds of the future, reflecting some of the ways in which these tools are used on the higher octaves of Light. The effectiveness of most of the techniques is largely dependent on the degree of spiritual attunement and capacity to use the "language of Light." The advanced awareness exercises presented above are invaluable in facilitating increasing degrees of mastery with the following techniques. As always, modify the guidelines according to inner guidance. Continue to explore these applications even if optimal results are not gained at first; for most, it will be a process of continuing unfolding in spiritual knowledge and abilities.

1. *Creating a crystal library:* Consider the possibility of programming appropriate crystals to act as extensions of the Universal Mind. These tools can be used to attract specific aspects of universal knowledge that can then be stored within the crystalline structure. Crystals of this nature function as resonating computer banks of information that are available for an individual to assimilate directly. If, for example,

knowledge is desired concerning sacred geometry, crystal technologies, the Great Pyramid, or healing, an archetype (7) or library crystal (8) can be so programmed and used as a cosmic "textbook." An entire library can be created using this idea with a number of crystals. The education process then takes on an entirely different "Light."

To create a crystal library, use the appropriate procedures to establish rapport with the crystal and spiritual attunement with higher-dimensional Light. In conjunction with Divine Intelligence, project the intention into the quartz-tool. After this, simply leave it in a positive and relatively isolated environment for a total of 3–5 days as it absorbs the desired information. Reinforce the programming once per day. Once the procedure is complete, project the awareness into the crystal and blend with the informational vibrations. Notice what images and color-sound patterns emerge in the mind. Most will find that this is not a linear process of education but more a superconscious and subconscious assimilation of ordered vibrations. When first using these library crystals, full recognition of the integrated knowledge will appear over time as it progressively shifts to conscious awareness. With practice, the recognition becomes more and more instantaneous. Working on a regular basis with this technique will facilitate this advancement.

2. *Decoding library and archetype crystals:* There are many crystals that have already been programmed with advanced knowledge by aspects of the Universal Mind and by ancient civilizations. Such storage houses of information await appropriate individuals to retrieve this "treasure." The skills required to decode such crystals are basically the same as those developed in the advanced awareness exercises and the use of the crystal library described above. As a library or archetype crystal of this nature is recognized, regularly project awareness into the crystal and blend with its energies. As discussed in the preceding section, the assimilation process is likely to be nonlinear. Continue integrating this knowledge on a daily basis, uniting the "mind" of the quartz into your own mind. Over time, layer after layer of new concepts, images, inventions,

and the like will come into conscious awareness. Much of our Divine heritage will be retrieved in this manner.

3. *Crystals as educational tools:* Crystals can be used as a primary tool in the educational process. The word *education* is employed here in a very broad sense to include the full spectrum of learning—from basic data to abstract principles to spiritual awareness. The main concept is that an appropriately programmed crystal can transfer the complex crystalline codings into the consciousness of a recipient. Such a tool can also transfer a specific aspect of an individual's consciousness to another person.

The children would sit on the floor and in front of them were patterns of crystals. . . . The crystals were all connected by copper rods placed underneath them. . . . From the corners of the rods were leads, copper leads. At the end of the lead was a coil, a flat copper coil which the child would place over their spiritual third eye. When the computers were placed in operation knowledge was dispensed from the computer into the crystals and into the individual's memory banks. Years of learning were placed inside of the mind in a matter of moments.[8]

The potentials within this facet of crystal technology are very far-reaching and open to much exploration within the parameters of spiritual guidance.

4. *Accelerated mental processes:* A crystal can be employed as a holographic computer that can carry out complex instructions and operations at very high speeds in conjunction with intellectual and creative pursuits. The computers of today operate at speeds far surpassing those of the human mind. The more advanced crystal computer goes beyond this as a multidimensional, lightning-fast extension of the human mind. In fact, the leading-edge technology of today is already working in this direction.

To date, the computer's power has been applied only to complex calculations or to simple, repetitive chores. That will not always be so. We will eventually build the first intelligence amplifier, a blend of computer and brain, optimizing both. We will link the brain and nervous system directly to the electronic computer, without the cumbersome keyboards, printers, and TV displays we use today. The computer will become not an antagonist but the ultimate extension of our reasoning, memory, and computational ability.[9]

Why wait 10–20 years for this next technological step when these future computers are in our hands today? Perhaps in this regard it is *consciousness* that needs to take the next step.

Programming is the keystone of higher-octave crystal usage. The application of this principle manifests the greatest potential of the crystal kingdom in conjunction with Divine Intelligence and human intention. It is for this reason that the foregoing programming section of this chapter is so relatively extensive and detailed. Indeed, without knowledge and skills in this realm, the use of crystals is only a dim reflection of what it can be. Therefore, use this part of the chapter as a workbook to come back to again and again to refine and expand your programming skills. For as spiritual intention aligns more and more with crystalline order, the interdimensional windows within our own consciousness open up to encompass greater degrees of the limitless vistas of celestial Light.

Crystal Gridwork Systems

Crystals placed in specific geometric patterns to produce a unified energy field are known as *gridwork systems*. These systems blend the energies of multiple crystals together to manifest a powerful synergistic effect. According to the principles of sacred geometry in conjunction with crystal and human energy dynamics, many different combinations can be formed to create specific effects. Such united crystals manifest an energy vortex area wherein a stronger resonating connection with higher octaves of Light is produced and maintained. Each individual quartz within the group can be programmed with particular energy frequencies; together, harmoniously integrated, programmed gridwork systems create strong geometric energy patterns. As a whole, they both provide an energetic framework of higher Light-intensities and maintain a spectrum of energy programs that may be drawn upon for specific Light-work done within them. These *multiple unity fields* are an environment unto themselves and, if used with insight, create an intermediate meeting ground between the earth-plane and the celestial realms.

The basic principle in creating gridwork systems is to place programmed crystals in harmonic patterns in which each crystal resonates strongly with every other. For better understanding, visualize a geometric webwork of energy lines going between all the crystals of the gridwork (see Figure 5). Their frequencies interact with each other just like the waves that emanate from several pebbles dropped in a pond. The intersections of these waves produce a dynamic energy mandala. The main idea in shaping various types of crystal gridworks is to form an energy mandala that most readily facilitates specific Light-work. This is to say, for example,

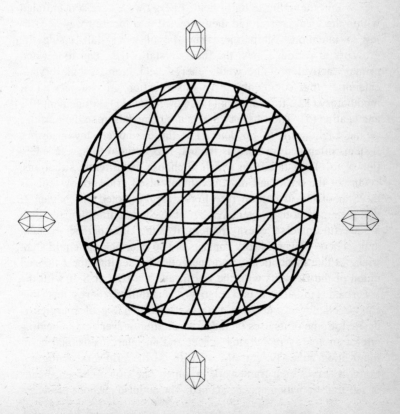

Figure 5: Gridwork System Energy Mandala

that interdimensional communication is better facilitated by a grid-work of a different configuration than that for the healing of the physical body. The challenge in this regard is to find crystals that suit the intended purpose, to program them, and then to set them in an optimal gridwork arrangement. The keys to achieving this are intuitive sensitivity, experience, and spiritual guidance. In the following material, some basic gridwork systems and guidelines are given as starting points for experience and experimentation. In working with these, others will evolve at later stages.

Within the dynamics of multiple crystal systems, it is very useful to have a *focal crystal*. This is a tool specifically selected and programmed to function as the primary uniter and director of energies within the multiple unity field. Energy waves are concentrated within the focal crystal and then directed in a focused way according to intention. While there may be other crystals inside the gridwork at various times, the focal crystal is the "capstone" and primary activator of the whole energy field. Some of the crystal categories that commonly serve this function are: surgery (15), modulatory (12), transmitting (11), power rods (1), attunement (3), and healing (5). The category that is used depends upon the purpose of the Light-work to be done. For those who employ gridwork systems often and for various intents, it is optimal to have a selection of focal crystals from which to choose for different situations.

One of the basic and most commonly used gridwork systems is the Star of David pattern (see Figure 6). As noted in Chapter 2, this pattern is both a potent symbol of the Judaic tradition and also a powerful universal energy pattern; it is the latter perspective that applies here. This gridwork consists of two interlocking, equidistant triangles that symbolically and energetically facilitate the balanced union of the Heavens with the Earth, and the Higher Self with the lower self. As such, it is a relatively generalized energy field that can be employed whenever a harmonious blending of energies is desired. Some of its uses include a meditation/prayer area, a healing circle, an energy recharging space, and an interdimensional communication zone. Essentially, as with all the gridwork configurations, it serves as a framework in which one's own chosen means of self-transformation may be applied. The outlined methods presented

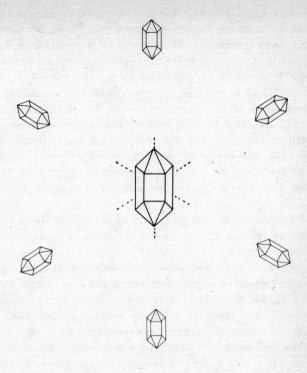

Figure 6: Star of David Crystal Gridwork System

below are given only as suggestions and guidelines that can be modified or put aside for other creative pursuits.

One healing technique that can be done with the Star of David pattern is as follows: Have an individual sit upright holding additional crystals in each hand. For this particular technique, the person should be situated with one of the gridwork's crystals directly in front and one directly in back. As the recipient begins to relax more and more deeply into a state of receptivity, the healing facilitator circles around the outside of the gridwork, using the focal crystal to pass over each of the outer crystals. This is to connect and unify the entire energy field and should be repeated a number of times in preparing for the healing work. Then, the facilitator channels healing vibrations through the focal crystal from outside the crystal pattern. After this cycle is complete, the facilitator then goes inside the gridwork and channels energies from this vantage point. In both of these steps, the energy is channeled from the front and back sides of the recipient. During the entire process, any number of specialized crystal healing techniques may be integrated as is felt appropriate. After this is completed, the facilitator leaves the circle and allows further energy dynamics to occur of their own accord. The recipient remains, receptively integrating the healing patterns until a cycle of completion is felt to occur. This healing method is a generalized one for the harmonization of all levels of the auric system. Through programming the Star of David crystals and the two crystals that are held in the hands, this process can be made more specific.

Another healing method involves infusing the six outer crystals with color rays an individual most needs and then placing them in a harmonic arrangement. The recipient sits in the center and is given a crystal to hold; this crystal is programmed to absorb auric imbalances. Once this segment is complete, it is taken by the facilitator and replaced by one programmed with specific healing energies. The recipient holds this crystal and allows it and the surrounding energy field to resonate within their being until the healing patterns have been absorbed and integrated, thus completing the treatment. This same technique can be used with quartz encoded with sound or a combination of color and sound.

For recharging one's own auric system, lay inside the gridwork with the head and feet directly in line with two opposite crystals. Place programmed crystals on the chakras, body areas, or meridian lines that need concentrated attention. Mentally connect the six surrounding crystals together and feel the resonation of the unified energy field as it blends more and more deeply with the aura and the crystals on the body. Breathe slowly and deeply, taking energy into the aura with the inhalation, holding the breath as your entire being is cleansed and energized, and then releasing imbalances and congestion with the out-breath. Continue this process along with any desired visualization methods until a cycle is ended. Then lay still and receptively resonate with the entire energy field for another period of time.

If interdimensional communication is the intent, one method of using the Star of David pattern is as follows: Program the crystals and place them into the gridwork arrangement. Sit upright with a focal crystal and mentally connect the surrounding crystals together until the whole system is activated. Blend with these resonations. Then concentrate into the focal crystal, feeling it to be the primary unifier of the energy field and the main communication tool. Focus the consciousness through this tool and establish a connection with the desired aspect(s) of the higher dimensions. Transmit your intention and then flow with the process of communication in whatever form of Light that it takes. The Star of David gridwork aids this procedure by establishing a stronger and more clarified interdimensional resonance through which such communication can occur.

Another gridwork system consists of twelve crystals in two interlocking, equidistant Star of David patterns (see Figure 7). It, too, is a relatively generalized energy field that can be modified for numerous purposes by varying the categories and programmings of the crystals that are employed. The combination of two Star of David gridworks adds greater intensities of Light due to the greater number of crystals. It also creates a more complex energy mandala that has a broader potential to be modified. This system in particular should be used with discretion and sensitivity, as overexposure over long periods of time can lead to potential imbalances. There is no need to be concerned with this possibility, though, as long as inner sensitivity is maintained. In the beginning it is best to start with an exposure time of less than ½ hour, then build up gradually to 45–60 minutes. The uses cited above for the Star of David pattern can also be applied with this one, along with other applications suggested further below.

A more specialized crystal pattern is one in which an individual lies down within a field of eight crystals (see Figure 8)—one directly above the head, one midway beneath the feet, and three on either side of the body at the knees, hips, and shoulders. Inside, place additional crystals on chakras, body areas, or meridian lines that need focused healing. This system is designed to equilibrate the total auric system and to repolarize and re-energize specific

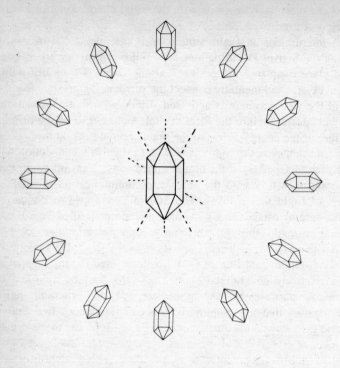

Figure 7: Twelve-Crystal Gridwork System

areas of imbalance. For self-healing, mentally connect the energy lines of the outer crystal pattern together and then align these energies with the aura and additional crystals. Slow, deep breathing along with suitable visualizations and deep relaxation will motivate the healing process in addition to other chosen techniques. This crystal gridwork can also be utilized by a healing facilitator in conjunction with various crystal healing methods presented in the healing section of this chapter.

A gridwork system created for the express purpose of interpersonal healing is done with six crystals in the shape of two elongated,

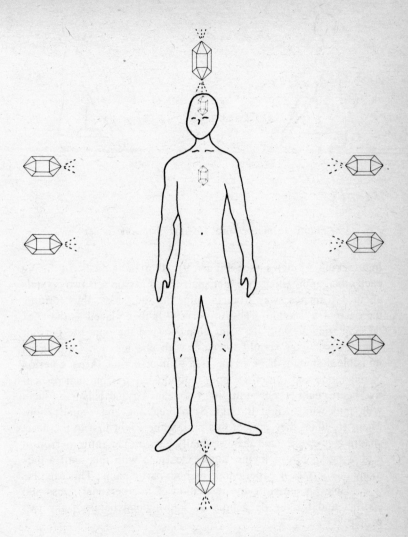

Figure 8: Eight-Crystal Healing Gridwork System

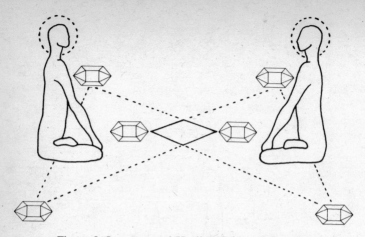

Figure 9: Interpersonal Healing Gridwork System

interlocking triangles (see Figure 9). Two individuals sit facing each other, approximately 3 feet apart. Each person sets two crystals about 3–6 inches away from the hips on both sides, thus forming the base of a triangle. The third crystal is then placed as the apex of each triangle with its point going toward the opposite person. The two triangles should intersect with one another, forming an invisible diamond shape in the area of intersection. After a period of relaxation and centering, both individuals focus on their respective heart chakras, concentrating on cleansing and balancing them with pink-white Light through deep breathing and visualization. Then, together, they project this pink-white Light first to the heart chakra of the other and then gradually envelop the entire person in a glowing sphere of loving Light. Continue with this until a harmony of energies is experienced by both participants. This exercise is valuable for assisting the resolution of interpersonal stress and conflict and for the deepening of a love bond between any two people.[10]

You are taking the energies of the trinity of one, and blending them with the energies of the trinity of another. The results will be ones of healing and releasing and of creating an understanding between the two. This pattern is extremely effective when utilized between two individuals whose spiritual vibrations are closely aligned and compatible, for it shall serve to unite them even closer.[11]

The pyramidal form can be integrated with crystal patterns in a number of ways, one of which is to suspend a pyramid above the twelve-crystal system at a height that is intuitively felt to be correct. Then attach copper, silver, or gold wiring from the crystals to the four corners of the pyramid; the wiring pattern goes from three consecutive crystals to the same pyramidal corner (see Figure 10). Also suspend a doubly terminated quartz within the pyramid itself at the height of the King's Chamber; a crystal attached to the apex will strengthen the energy field, too. The effect created is an extremely potent unified field that can, among other things, function as a personal initiation chamber. Basically, it is an energy vortex that resonates strongly with higher-dimensional pyramidal-crystal vortexes. It can also be employed as a very effective interdimensional communication chamber. Overall, it is best used with discretion, guided by spiritual awareness.

In addition to the above ideas and guidelines, there are many other concepts to be explored:

1. A twelve-crystal pattern can function as an outer gridwork that surrounds another gridwork system. The inner pattern can be changed to suit varying situations and intent. The combination of these two configurations can magnify the total energy field onto a higher octave of effectiveness.

2. At various key intersection points within the energy mandala of a gridwork, additional crystals and/or precious stones can be placed to both modify and amplify the unified field for particular purposes.

3. Crystal clusters (multiple crystals physically united) can be used in the same basic manner as single crystals. The energy dynamics of clusters, though, work somewhat differently. Although each specific crystal within the grouping can be programmed separately, it continues to send its energy lines out in a distinct direction. The entire cluster, then, sends out numerous energy lines from a single location, therefore making the whole energy mandala much more complex. A gridwork of clusters can be orchestrated to focus multiple energy lines

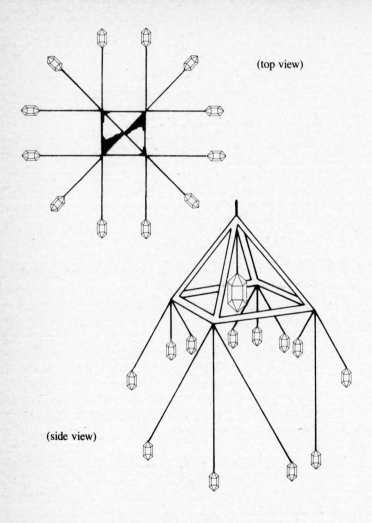

(top view)

(side view)

Figure 10: Pyramid-Crystal Initiation Chamber

into desired locations. In healing, for example, such a grid-work could focus concentrated energies on several specific areas at once for more potent results. Thus clusters add another dimension to the gridwork concept. This will be explained in more depth in the crystal clusters section of this chapter.

4. Other geometric shapes can be used as the pattern for a crystal system—hexagons, spirals, squares, octagons, rectangles, and so on. Each will have its own distinct mandalic energy pattern with which to experiment.

5. A pyramid placed over each crystal in the Star of David or twelve-crystal system will modify these gridworks into even more effective interdimensional communication chambers.

6. Using copper, silver, or gold wiring to connect the gridwork crystals together is an excellent way of enhancing the energy flow of the entire system. To do this, wrap the wiring 1–3 times around each crystal so that all are linked into a complete circuit.

7. Gridwork patterns can be extended three-dimensionally by placing crystals at harmonic locations within an entire room. One of the key areas in a room is the corners, both on ground and ceiling levels. The tendency of 90-degree corners is to keep energy fairly static. By placing crystals in the ground level corners pointing upward and in the ceiling level corners pointing to the center of the room, the energy flow is made more kinetic. Other crystals set at various heights along the walls with tips directed into the room and on the ceiling with tips focused downwards will amplify the 3–D gridwork. These locations in conjunction with patterns on the floor can manifest a very dynamic force field.

8. A group of people working closely together with the same intention can augment the power and effectiveness of their Light-work by sitting at harmonic intervals within a multiple-crystal system.

9. Work done in gridworks can be amplified by accompanying it with suitable sonic frequencies, music, color, and aromas.

10. Mirrors placed on the walls around a gridwork system at key regions will reflect and amplify the energy dynamics. This

is best done by locating the mirrors directly opposite to one another and focusing the angle of reflection into the center of the energy mandala. Geometric mirror patterns placed in this way are optimal.

11. Programmed crystal patterns placed around a plant are helpful in establishing a deeper communication with the vibratory realms of the plant kingdom. By sitting in front of a plant and projecting awareness into the plant-crystal energy field, the channels of communication are broadened and clarified.

Healing with Crystals

Healing, in general, is the harmonizing of imbalanced energy fields toward their inherently perfect state of functioning. All levels of the auric system have an innate momentum to maintain homeostatic balance and to synergize in evolutionary advancement. Disease occurs when the underlying intelligence of the auric system is impeded by imbalanced energy patterns, thereby creating a state of dissonance and subsequent disorder. Healing consists of emphasizing the natural resonant frequencies of a harmonious energy field and thereby returning it to its original order. When vibrations of health are accentuated, the resonance with the auric system's inherent equilibrium either disperses dissonant energies or synchronizes them with the harmonious frequencies. Essentially, balance resonates with balance and creates a situation in which imbalance cannot occur. The role of a healing facilitator is to neutralize discordant interference with homeostasis and to emphasize the already-existing blueprint of perfection.

Crystal healing, in particular, employs the capabilities of quartz to receive, retain, modify, and transmit an extremely broad range of complex energy frequencies in conjunction with its sensitive responsiveness to thought-waves of Divine Intelligence and the human mind. Indeed, while crystals are but one tool of healing among many, their distinctive properties are as multidimensional connectors and as intelligent computers programmed to perform myriad precise functions. These two basic characteristics make quartz crystals a healing modality unto themselves and a cooperative synergetic agent with other healing methodologies. Crystals exemplify the essence of healing with their precise, symmetrical patterns and resonating, balanced order. As these qualities are projected from the crystal into the auric system, order reverberates with order, pattern with pattern, harmony with harmony, till the energies are one, and health inevitably resounds.

Within these essential principles, many modes of application are possible. In the following material, many techniques will be presented and seed-thoughts planted. In lieu of elaborately describing every procedure and exploring every thought in explicit detail, guidelines and potentials are given in the hope of encouraging each individual to find those modifications and innovations that best suit every unique person and situation. The patterns of creativity and healing abilities manifest differently through each one of us; and while certain fundamental properties of healing and crystal dynamics exist, there is great room for variation and experimentation within these predominating themes.

1. To re-energize the body and quicken the spirit, place the main facet of a crystal on a principal pulse area. This can be done with multiple crystals on a corresponding number of pulse areas at the same time. Doing this technique in direct sunlight, drawing the sun's rays into the auric system through the crystal(s), is optimally effective. This can be done either for self-healing or as a method employed by a healing facilitator. Be careful not to press very hard on the pulse areas, especially the carotid arteries; only gentle contact is needed.

2. For general re-energizing, place crystals on both wrists with points toward the body, and concentrate on drawing energy into the entire body while sitting in direct outdoor sunlight. This exercise is particularly effective using long, slender, clear crystals. If a specific body area or chakra needs additional energy, put a crystal there and draw sunlight into this location through the crystalline structure. Employing gridwork systems as a sun focalizer for healing and self-transformation is also another means of applying this technique.

3. To aid in dispelling cramps and specific areas of tension and disharmony, program a charged crystal to absorb imbalances, lay it on the desired location and feel it drawing these energies into itself. After this is completed, place another crystal on the same location for 5–10 minutes to infuse it with positive healing energies.

4. For alleviating headaches, one method found to be successful is to place the base of a crystal against the main area of pain with the point directed outward. Visualize and feel the stress being pulled out of the head through the crystal and being dispelled. Another technique is to utilize a crystal programmed to absorb imbalances set on the painful area and gently covered with the left hand. Hold it there until the disharmony dissipates.

5. The healing of the physical body can be assisted through *bio-programming*. This entails programming a distinct image of a body area or body system into a crystal and then incorporating the image into the physical body. This procedure can be used to facilitate wholeness in any disorder, from broken bones to lymphatic congestion to glandular imbalances. In the programming process, it is usually helpful to have an anatomy and physiology text at hand to help increase the clarity and accuracy of the encoded image. Visualize this mental picture holographically from many angles, and surround it with pure white Light, allowing Divine Intelligence to assist in the entire process. Next, put the crystal on the body part or at a central juncture of the body system for 5–10 minutes, feeling the perfect energy pattern resonate within the body with meditative sensitivity. Then remove the crystal and reinforce the programming for 30–60 seconds and replace it to the original location, repeating the same process as before. Continue this procedure for as many cycles as necessary. Though this method is not meant to replace other appropriate forms of health care, it can serve as a very effective adjunct in reinforcing and quickening the healing process when done on a regular basis.

6. A quartz pendulum can be used to harmonize the aura through its ability to detect and mend such imbalances. Mentally

divide the body into five vertical lines, the middle line extending along the axis of the spine. The next two lines on either side of the body are at the shoulders, and the last two are 5–6 inches further apart. Take the pendulum and move it slowly along each of the imaginary lines. When it starts to move of its own accord, an imbalance is indicated. Hold the pendulum steady at this location and allow it to swing freely until the motion gradually stops. This signifies that the healing of this area is finished. Continue onwards until another imbalance is detected, following the same procedure through all five vertical lines.

7. For a quick ''tune-up'' of the body's meridian lines, take a doubly terminated crystal and place it between the thumb and forefinger. Twirl it with the opposite hand for 30–60 seconds. Repeat the same process for each succeeding finger, using the thumb as a fulcrum point. Once these steps have been completed with one hand, duplicate the same procedure with the other one.

8. In homeopathy, silica is used as a strengthener and eliminator.

   This substance, which belongs to Sagittarius, has the property of attracting light and driving out evil. . . . Silicic acid imparts self-confidence, strengthens the back (especially the intervertebral discs), promotes the discharge of water, pus, and all superfluous and undesirable materials and protects the nerves.[12]

9. For faster healing of skin tissue—scars, acne, rashes, and so on—expose a crystal to sunlight for 2–4 hours and immediately lay it on the skin for 15–30 minutes. Do this 1–3 times per day during the entire healing process.

10. Crystals can be utilized to balance the body's meridian lines by gently tracing them directly over these energy avenues. Place the crystal's main facet on the skin and slide it lightly over the meridian line, back and forth, until the energies are flowing smoothly and harmoniously. For localized areas of imbalance, rub the crystals in a concentrated manner in these regions, and then trace the entire length of the meridian to facilitate full equilibrium.

11. The vibrational quality of water can be significantly increased with crystals. To make ''crystal water,'' place a

crystal in a clear jar full of water and place it outside for 24 hours. The water serves as a receptive medium that stores the energy of the crystal as it processes the energies of the sun, moon, and stars. This charged fluid can be utilized in countless ways—drinking, watering plants, washing the skin, rinsing wounds, and so on. The increased vibrations of the water will be transferred in its application, thus making greater intensities of Light available to be assimilated. In particular, drinking crystal water on a regular basis will gradually increase the vibrational quality of every cell. Approximately 70 percent of the body is water; it is the medium in which the great majority of metabolic processes take place. Crystal water brings added Light to these metabolic reactions and, as a result, the entire auric system is vibrationally upgraded. An especially good time to drink this fluid is immediately before and after healing and self-transformation processes to integrate their effects more fully. In addition, a specific color vibration that is needed can be enhanced in the making of crystal water by placing a piece of translucent colored gel or plastic around the jar or with a crystal programmed with a certain color vibration.

12. Crystals are able to modify and amplify the transfer of healing energy from one person to another. In the realm of the "healing touch," research has shown that the right and left hands produce noticeable and distinct effects. The left palm produces a calming, soothing, and healing energy, while the right palm generates an activating and strengthening effect. Stated from another perspective, the left hand is yin, receptive, and "negative," and the right hand is yang, active, and "positive." Each hand has specific applications according to the nature of a situation. For example, inflamed and aggravated conditions can be soothed and assuaged by placing the left palm over the area; devitalized and stagnant conditions can be activated and energized by applying the right palm on the region. Conversely, it would *not* be beneficial to apply the soothing effect of the left palm on a congested, underactive condition that needs the activation of the right hand; nor would the strengthening energies of the

right hand be suitable for calming the agitation of a headache or other overactive situations when the soothing of the opposite hand is needed. Furthermore, both hands can be used together, one placed on top of the other, to create a more powerful, synergistic effect. For this, put the primary hand over the affected area and then place the other hand directly on top, thus making a complete "circuit." The same effect can be produced by applying the primary hand on the area to be healed and the secondary hand on the opposite side of the body.[13] In conjunction with crystals, these healing energies can be amplified for more pronounced results. Place a selected crystal in the correct hand with the point toward the fingertips. Apply the hand to the specified area, resting it comfortably on top of the crystal and adjoining skin area. Attune to Divine Intelligence and allow the flow of healing energies to occur for as long as needed. After this process is finished, put another crystal on the area and have the recipient remain in a receptive state for 5–15 minutes, assimilating and integrating the energy patterns that were received.

13. "Crystals can be used to cleanse and energize acupuncture needles. Pour distilled water in a glass bowl, gently place the crystals then the acupuncture needles in the water, let them remain for about 12 minutes."[14]

14. Research has shown that the right palm placed on the medulla oblongata (lower part of the back of the head) while the left palm is applied to the forehead creates an increase in strength and well-being.[15] This effect is magnified by using an appropriate crystal in each hand.

15. Experimentation has demonstrated that the breathing process can be used to regulate the concentration and projection of crystal energies. The inhalation brings energy into the auric system. By holding the breath for 3–6 seconds and focusing awareness into a crystal in hand, this energy can be concentrated and centralized within the quartz itself. With a forced, rapid out-breath the accumulated energy is projected out through the top of the crystal with intensified force. By pointing a crystal at a specific area in need of healing and using several cycles of the above breathing sequence, pow-

erful bursts of energy can be directed into the desired region. For healing on the spiritual, mental, and emotional levels, locate the area of the body that is the focal point on the physical level for this imbalance. Point the crystal at this area when employing this technique.

16. A self-healing method using the breathing process in a similar manner is as follows: Lay down comfortably and place a crystal on a chakra that needs to be better balanced. With the inhalation place both hands on top of the crystal and draw energy through it into the chakra. Hold the breath for 3–6 seconds and concentrate the energy deeply within this region. Exhale forcefully, dispersing negative energy patterns out of the chakra in a quick burst. At the same time, move the arms rapidly out to the side of the body, coinciding with the exhalation. With the next slow, deep inhalation, gradually bring the hands back to the crystal to start another sequence. Repeat several cycles of this procedure until the healing process is complete.

17. A healing practitioner who is adept in the programming of crystals can use that ability to encode them for clients to carry on a regular basis or to employ with certain suggested self-healing techniques that will reinforce the healing work done in sessions with the practitioner.

18. Holding a crystal in each hand will help to exchange and balance the male and female energies within the individual. This is a good method that can be utilized as an adjunct in a wide variety of healing modalities. The recipient of the healing sessions can simply hold the crystals while other techniques are being done. Another excellent time to use this idea is during meditation and other self-transformation work.

19. Marcel Vogel, a noted crystal practitioner in San Jose, California, reports that crystals can be used as projectors of the vibrations of homeopathic substances and Bach Flower remedies. A drop of water is placed on the very top of the crystal, and a very small amount of the appropriate agent is put into the water. As a deep inhalation is taken in and held for a few seconds, awareness is focused on the crystal held in the hand. Pointing it to the desired location, a forceful

exhalation projects the vibrations of the remedy, and the process is complete.[16]

This same technique has also been used by others with gem tinctures, vitamins, and herbs.

20. For use in the healing touch and the various forms of body-work, the hands can be charged up to a high degree by rolling a crystal back and forth between both hands for 45–60 seconds. This procedure is helpful in preparation for healing work and also for building up a charge to infuse into body areas that need focused attention.

21. A self-transformation technique for general energization and stimulation is done by putting crystals on each of the chakras, including the Alpha and Omega chakras. Then do the meditation exercise described at the end of Chapter 4 that resonates pyramidal energy dynamics with the human auric system.

22. One method of generating an energy charge in a crystal in preparation for use is to slide the thumb in an up-and-down motion on several of the top facets and sides for approximately 45–60 seconds.

23. Groupings of crystals can be applied in specific patterns on and around the body to facilitate the healing of particular conditions. The basic principle for this healing modality is to focus the energy patterns of two or more crystals on an area in need of healing. For example, with a broken leg, put one crystal on either side of the break with the points toward each other. These two crystals (as with all others that might be used) emanate their primary energies through the points and thereby concentrate increased healing energy to the specified location. For various conditions, specialized gridworks can be constructed on the body itself and/or immediately around it. For example, to activate a sluggish liver, it is beneficial to place a miniature Star of David gridwork around the liver region with the crystal points toward the center. To eliminate a negative energy pattern from the liver, create a similar Star of David gridwork, except with the points away from the center, thus helping to disperse the undesired energies. These and other crystal placements can be adapted to

any health imbalance according to the principles of adding healing energy by pointing the crystals toward the affected area and dispersing negative patterns by pointing them away from the focal region.

Here are a few examples of such applications:

For a headache, place a gridwork of six crystals on the floor around the head with the points outward. Two of them are put at ear level and the rest at equidistant points encompassing the head. The recipient can optionally hold another crystal at the third eye with point outward.

With a sluggish colon, set numerous crystals on the abdomen directly over the colon area with the points in the direction of elimination.

For depression, surround the entire body with up to twenty-four crystals at equidistant intervals with points inward. Also put a crystal at each of the chakras, including the Alpha and Omega crystal chakras. Have the recipient do long, deep breathing and visualization of white Light coming into and energizing the auric system. Next, turn the points of all the surrounding crystals outward, and the recipient then consciously expels negative energy patterns. Finally, turn all the points inward and once again employ deep breathing and positive visualization.

With a sore throat, for example, put six crystals on the floor level, three on each side at equidistant intervals with the points inward. Place two more on the body just above and below the throat, pointing toward this area. Visualize a soothing color, such as blue, infusing the area with each inhalation.

For concentrated work on a specific chakra, set a six- or twelve-crystal gridwork around the area with points inward. Employ suitable breathing, visualization, and any other appropriate healing methods to assimilate healing energies. Next, turn all the points outward and proceed to consciously dissipate negative energies. Finally, turn the points back to their original position and repeat the healing techniques used before.

These and many other applications and adaptations are possible for all the myriad varieties of health imbalances. Simply apply these basic principles and use them in conjunction with other appropriate healing modalities—color therapy, bodywork, aromatherapy, sonics, and so on. For additional information on specific gridworks and crystal placements for particular disease conditions, refer to *Exploring Atlantis, Vol. 2*, by Rev. Dr. Frank Alper.

24. For general healing and vibratory enhancement of the chakras, rotate a crystal with the point toward the body in front of each chakra for 30–60 seconds, starting from the lowermost and going to the top. After completing the rotations at each energy center, hold it steady and be receptive to the harmonizing that occurs.

    Another similar technique is to trace an elongated ellipse, going from the lowermost to the uppermost chakras and back down again in slow sweeps. The plane of this ellipse is parallel to the body. Continue with this motion for 2–3 minutes.

25. A crystal placed over the heart chakra with both hands on top of it will key a significant amount of balancing and transmutation of the entire auric system. This process can be enhanced with deep-breathing exercises, creative visualization, and other suitable self-transformation methods.

26. Crystal energies are stimulated by the movement of water and thereby function as excellent adjuncts in the various applications of hydrotherapy. Crystals placed in the main flow of water and/or held on a particular body part that is the primary focus of the treatment will add significant energy to the healing process.

27. Within the modality of aromatherapy, crystals programmed with specific fragrances and placed on a body area for healing purposes can be employed in conjunction with the olfactory vibrations of the identical aroma. Used together, the encoded crystal vibrations plus the fragrance itself can create a strong synergistic effect.

28. For the more advanced healing practitioner, a gridwork of crystals placed on the body in specific configurations can be used to balance and charge the glandular systems of the physical body. The key is to put the gridworks at key junctures of glandular functioning. For example, to harmonize an imbalanced relationship between the pituitary gland and the adrenal glands, program three crystals with appropriate tones, colors, and thought-images. Put one directly above the head, pointing into the pituitary gland; put the other ones on top of the adrenals, both pointing upwards toward the head. During the treatment, use sound tones and colors to accompany the healing action of the crystals. With the lymphatic system, as another example, place crystals at all the primary lymph-node regions, with the points toward the direction of the lymphatic fluid circulation. Charge them with white Light before setting them on the body. This can best be done with a slide projector. When they are in place, use a projector to shine the full spectrum of colors, one at a time, on the entire body, spending more time on those colors that need to be emphasized for a particular condition. Continue this procedure for a full 45–50-minute healing session.

29. The blending of color, sound, and crystals is potentially one of the most powerful healing combinations. As more and more knowledge evolves concerning each of these elements, ways of uniting them in precise energy patterns for complete healing in a single therapy session will occur. The energy field of a specific body organ, for example, can be duplicated through the exact synthesis of particular tones, color frequencies, and programmed crystals. When this field is superimposed upon the body organ, it is re-organized within the form of the perfect energy pattern.

Now, it follows in this manner, when an aberration in vibrations has been ascertained, and a specific ailment has been established. By utilizing your crystals in the proper formations. By bathing them in the proper color for healing in that area, and for that disease, and evoking the vibrations of the sound or note, all at the same time, you create the harmony of vibrations that are in total compatability with the organic structure. An instantaneous healing shall be effected.[17]

At this point in time, much experimentation needs to be done toward this goal. Some ideas for this include:

Place crystals on all the chakras and shine various colors onto them simultaneously. Note the differences and similarities between the effects of each color. Try the same procedure with specific tones or music sequences. For this, it is helpful to place a speaker directly above the head and below the feet at the horizontal level of the crystals on the body. Once a groundwork of knowledge is gained, then apply combinations of both color and sound.

Create gridwork systems composed of color- and sound-programmed crystals. Try different arrangements and various color and sound combinations.

A simpler and more directly applicable technique consists of putting a crystal programmed with a color vibration on a body area or chakra and shining the same color on this area. A very effective healing session can be done by using this basic principle on each chakra in turn. Discern what color vibration each chakra needs the most and program a separate crystal for each one with this frequency. During the healing session, work with one energy center at a time, putting the encoded crystal in place and shining the corresponding color on this location also. Spend about 5–6 minutes on every area. This same process can be done with musical tones in place of colors in an identical fashion.

30. The effects of bodywork of many kinds—massage, neuromuscular therapy, acupressure, polarity therapy, and so on—can be magnified through creative applications of crystal concepts.

The healing practitioner can augment the healing energies that flow through his or her auric system into the recipient by having crystals on key body areas. For generalized amplification, wearing or carrying a personal crystal is useful. To aid in the flow of energies through the hands, small doubly terminated crystals can either be strapped to the middle of the wrists or held in place by wristbands. If single-terminations are used, the points are turned toward the fingertips. For specialized healing work emanating from the facilitator's throat or third-eye centers, a crystal can be kept in place with a necklace or headband, respectively.

Gridwork systems placed under and/or around the therapy area will significantly enhance the overall vibrational intensities. Specialized gridworks can be created to resonate with the needs of particular individuals receiving treatments.

Relatively small (½–3 inches) crystals can be glued to the underside of a massage table in a gridwork arrangement. This configuration can consist of up to 20–30 crystals placed in a generalized gridwork.

If oil or lotion is used, a charged crystal can be placed in the solution, thereby activating it with greater Light.

If a particular area of the recipient's body needs focused attention, a crystal can be put on this region beforehand to prepare it for healing work and then afterward to help integrate these energies. This can be made even more effective by placing a warm towel, heat pack, or herbal fomentation over the crystal during this time.

A long, slender crystal can be lightly rolled on the recipient's body for generalized healing and vibrational enhancement. This technique should be totally painless and for this reason a crystal that is faceted to have twelve sides is optimal; otherwise, carefully choose one that can be used without discomfort to the recipient. This procedure is excellent as a beginning and ending routine.

31. Crystal healing techniques can be incorporated into those healing modalities that do not directly involve crystals. For example, a crystal can be programmed to assimilate the healing patterns that occur during a healing session. It can then be kept in close proximity between sessions to reinforce the healing process. Also, during the last 5–10 minutes of a treatment, various crystal techniques may be utilized that are complementary to the primary modality being used. The ways that crystals can be employed as an adjunct in other

realms of healing are multitudinous, limited only by creative initiative.

Spiritual Activation and Alignment Through Crystal Technologies

The concepts of spiritual activation and alignment are significantly different from what is normally regarded as health and healing. *Health* is commonly used to denote the balanced and efficient functioning of the human auric system, and *healing* is used to characterize the process of correcting any imbalance therein. From this point of view, a physically balanced, well-adjusted, productive person is healthy. Numerous other health-care systems and spiritual disciplines regard these concepts in a more encompassing way. These perspectives see man as a potentially perfect and unlimited being of infinite creative abilities, and anything less than the full realization of this potential is not optimal health and requires healing in order to attain this ultimate state. Both of these viewpoints are true within their conceptual frame of reference. From a relative point of view, there is no contradiction between the two; each deals with a specified realm of human functioning, experience, and potential. *Spiritual activation and alignment*, on the other hand, are used here as qualitatively different concepts. *Activation* is the process of catalyzing accelerated evolutionary growth, usually involving a quantitative and qualitative shift in the degree of conscious attunement with the Higher Self and the Universal Mind. *Alignment* is defined as the integrating and balancing of all levels of the auric system during the activation process. While activation is concerned with stimulating rapid development of higher-octave capabilities, alignment deals with the balanced integration and functioning of this activated potential. Both factors are equally important in this accelerated growth process. Activation without corresponding alignment bears scattered and imbalanced energies; alignment without corresponding activation bears integrated but relatively dormant spiritual faculties. These concepts, then, add a new perspective to consider as a new era of consciousness transformation rapidly unfolds in the coming years.

The *creative moment* is the precise instant of activation and alignment into greater degrees of communication, or communion, with the Light-body and the Universal Mind. As we approach the Omega point, or "ending" period, of an evolutionary cycle, the potential for this process increases exponentially. This moment is one in which celestial Light shines through the veils surrounding the Earth-plane like a laser beam through fog. It can be envisioned as the infusion of higher-octave Light-codings into the auric DNA grid system, thus catalyzing a respatialization, or recrystallization, process into a higher-dimensional energy pattern. What is sometimes known as the New Age is nothing less than a quantum dimensional transformation of consciousness into the fourth-dimensional Light-body. This culminating "creative moment" will be brought about by crystal-based Light-technologies of the ancient past and the near future. As in the highly advanced civilizations of the past where Divine Science was utilized for spiritual activation and alignment, so also today this knowledge is resurfacing and being applied in progressive steps to facilitate a graceful evolvement into the Light-body. While techniques and technologies toward this end are not presented in this text for considered reasons, the authors have manifested, and continue to further develop, Light-based therapies for this express purpose. (See "About the Authors" on page 159.)

Crystal Wands

Crystal wands have been used throughout the centuries as tools for communication and projection of power. From the wizard's staff to the high priest's breastplate to the Atlantean crystal laser, wands of many varieties and technical levels have been created. Manifestations of this concept often reflect advanced degrees of knowledge concerning the inherent Light-properties of quartz. Essentially, these devices function as finely tuned extensions of the self used to augment higher-octave spiritual capabilities. The large majority of such tools involves the blending of refined metals with quartz. This union serves to enlarge the scope of crystal applications in the technological realms. The crystal wands of today and tomorrow reflect advancing degrees of knowledge in the Divine Sciences of crystal energetics and metallurgy.

Four major metals are utilized for their discrete properties—gold, silver, copper, and lead. Though it is beyond the scope of this book to delve into the complexities of such an advanced science, it is suitable here to present an overview of their predominant qualities. *Gold* functions as a superior receptor and processor of energy waves. The assimilation and processing of these energies is then passed on to the crystal. Gold is the capstone of the metal kingdom, while quartz is the capstone of the gem kingdom; together, used side by side, they are a standard unit of Light-perfection, functioning as a quintessential paragon of communication. It is important to note, in this regard, that in crystal wands the most productive way of employing these two elements is in direct energetic contact with each other. *Copper*, on the other hand, is a metal of transference and modulation. This element is the ''sister'' of electricity on the metaphysical level. Well known for its ability to transfer electrical currents, copper performs the same function for higher-octave energy spectrums. Also, as used in crystal wands, it can modify energy frequencies very precisely, dependent on the number of revolutions of wiring around another element or the length of copper tubing. These variables create harmonic intervals that can be used to fine-tune the overall harmonics of a crystal wand. *Silver*, too, is known for its highly conductive properties. In addition to transfering energies it also increases the vibratory pitch of the frequencies that pass through it. In relationship to copper, silver is able to modify the higher-energy octaves to a considerably finer degree while the primary influence of copper is in the lower octaves; in this regard, they cooperate synergistically throughout the myriad spectrums of energy. Lastly, *lead* is the harmonic opposite of silver. Its properties are those of grounding and dampening of vibrations. In conjunction with the other metals, a specific amount and configuration of lead can decrease vibrational frequencies when the overall harmonics are not fully aligned; lead also amalgamates and grounds scattered energies. These four fundamental metals, then, expand the spectrum of crystal applications, serving to modify and fine-tune the Light of quartz into advanced technical formats.

Presented herein are four examples of crystal wands to be applied and used as stepping-stones toward further improvements and innovations:

1. *Auric amplifying pendant* (Figure 11): This is a pendant similar to some of the more advanced amulets and talismans worn by ancient priests and priestesses. For optimal results, it must be tuned to an individual's unique vibratory patterns by selecting and programming a suitable crystal, using the type of

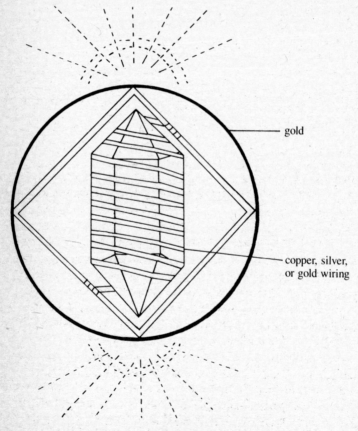

gold

copper, silver, or gold wiring

Figure 11: Auric Amplifying Pendant

metal (copper, silver, or gold) that is most appropriate, and by winding the metal wire in precise harmonic ratios. This tool will greatly amplify the auric system in general in the manner of a personal crystal when worn as a pendant over the heart chakra. For further applications, it can be taken in hand and placed in front of the third eye for communication and energy transmissions, used as a focal crystal in gridwork systems and as a tool of healing. Structurally, it consists of a circle enclosing a diamond shape set according to the angles of the Great Pyramid (approximately 51 degrees at the corners and 76 degrees at the apexes); both the circle and diamond are made of gold. Within this structure, a doubly terminated crystal is set into place with both ends terminating in the pyramidal apexes. Around the crystal is copper, silver, or gold wiring wrapped to resonate with the individual's harmonic vibratory level. This device can be modified to suit a large percentage of individuals, who will find it to be a most useful tool of self-transformation.

2. *Communication wand* (Figure 12): This instrument is analogous to a radio transmitting tower except that it can process and project more complex energies in broader spectrums of applications. A very precise and responsive "tuning fork," it serves as a highly effective means of transmitting and receiving telethought communication. Within a very powerful energy field created technologically, such a device could serve as an interdimensional communications tower. As illustrated, the crystal is connected on both ends to silver rods of small diameter, molded into a partial circle on top and a partial ellipse on the bottom. The diameter, angles, and sizes of the silver rods are tuning variables. The crystal itself is doubly terminated and programmed for its function. In addition, numerous facets are carved with individual-specific symbolic configurations and packed with gold in order to reinforce and modify the crystal's programming. Copper, silver, or gold wiring is wrapped around the junction points between the silver rods and the crystal terminations. In use, the two ends of the lower rods are held in each hand and positioned in front

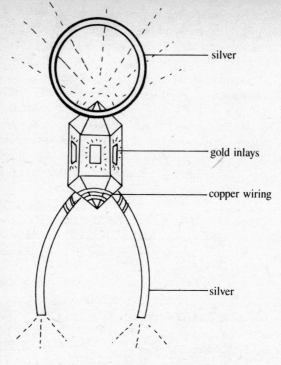

silver

gold inlays

copper wiring

silver

Figure 12: A Communication Wand

of the third-eye region; thought transmissions are then sent and received.

3. *Crystal amplification chamber* (Figure 13): This chamber is designed to transmit thoughts and energies programmed into a crystal by an individual or to activate an encoded archetype or library crystal and to transmit these codes on an amplified wavelength. The former application is like a radionics device that continually emanates its programmed energies into the surrounding environment. Essentially it is an amplification device in this regard. In the latter application, the function is more of the activation of dormant coded knowledge and its subsequent transmission in an amplified and clarified format.

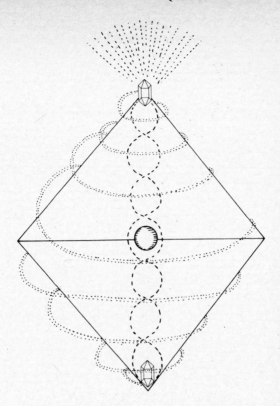

Figure 13: Crystal Amplification Chamber

The framework is composed of two pyramids bonded together at their respective bases to form an octahedron. Each pyramid is made of silver with gold plating. The crystal to be activated and amplified is placed in the lower apex; another crystal functions as the upper capstone but acts only as part of the octahedral unit itself. The outside of the octahedron is strung with silver wire in both clockwise and counterclockwise directions according to the ratio of phi (1:1.618 . . .). In the exact middle of the octahedron an appropriately programmed small crystal ball or doubly terminated crystal can be strung into place. In use, it is very helpful to charge and activate the primary crystal as much as possible before placing it in the lower apex. Once it is set inside, the chamber works of its own accord, though with additional energy input such as focused thought-energy or a laser beam, the transmissions will be stronger.

4. *Crystal Ankh* (Figure 14): This device unites the Light of quartz with the archetypal symbol of the key of eternal life. As it was utilized in ancient times, the ankh served as a wand, a projector of energies. With a crystal incorporated into its structure, its inherent powers are more strongly activated and it becomes a more powerful and responsive tool for

Figure 14: Crystal Ankh

healing, self-transformation, and communication. Structurally, it is simply a matter of placing a doubly terminated crystal within the upper loop of the ankh. Copper, silver, or gold wiring is wrapped around the crystal to tune it more precisely to the individual user. Optionally, a number of the crystal's facets and sides can be carved with specific symbols and packed with gold to attune it even more exactly. Another option is to inlay smaller faceted crystals at various intervals within the ankh itself.

These examples of crystal wands encompass but a tiny percentage of the possible applications. They, and others, are forerunners of grand technologies beyond current dreams. Presented below are two examples of such Light-based technologies.

As a scientific instrument it was used in conjunction with a complex system of mirrors of pure gold, reflectors and lenses to produce healing in the bodies of those who were inside the Temple of Light. . . . When the Disc was struck by a priest-scientist, who understood its operation, it would set certain vibratory conditions which could even bring about great earthquakes and, if continued long enough, might bring about a change in the rotation of the Earth itself. When attuned to a person's particular frequency pattern it could transport this person wherever he wished to go merely by the mental picture he created. It was, therefore, an object of transportation.

The Golden Sun Disc of Mu was not made of ordinary gold, but was transmuted, and unusual in its qualities in that it was a translucent metal. . . .[18]

The crystals used in the laser surgery . . . were encased inside a coil like structure. . . . The copper coil was connected to a highly sophisticated bank of computers. When the proper frequency of energy was determined in relation to the specific disease, or problem that existed, these vibrations passed through the coil into the crystal through leads attached at the rear termination. A force field was erected between the coil and the crystal to contain the energy throughout the length of the crystal, building intensities, ending in the forward termination to be imparted to the individual under treatment at that time. The energy frequency was totally compatible with the energies of the diseased organ, effecting a total cure. The frequencies of color and tonal sound were blended with the tissue frequencies to totally re-align the energy patterns of the physical structure.[19]

Cocreating with Crystals

The world is your exercise-book, the pages on which you do your sums.
It is not reality, although you can express reality there if you wish. You
are also free to write nonsense, or lies, or to tear the pages.[10]

Within Divine Order, we have the capacity to become conscious
cocreators with Divine Intelligence in the process of manifesting
events, objects, and lessons into our lives. Through focused intention, a high charged thought-form is created that will manifest
according to the law of cause and effect. In this context, crystals
can amplify thought signals to connect them more strongly with the
causal levels of Light. Therefore, they act as windows through
which we may exercise our powers of cocreation more directly and
efficiently. In so doing, we become more and more aware that *all*
aspects of our individual lives are chosen.

The mark of your ignorance is the depth of your belief in injustice and
tragedy. What the caterpillar calls the end of the world, the master calls a
butterfly.[21]

With increased cocreative abilities the double-edged sword of
greater awareness comes to bear. As crystals help open the windows
of consciousness to the more causal dimensions, all intentions put
forth will manifest in precise detail. A wise, old saying applies
here—''Be careful what you ask for, you may very well get it!''
Spiritual discernment becomes an increasingly crucial factor in
choosing the direction and content our our lives. And this is exactly
the reason for uniting awareness with Divine Intelligence when
programming a crystal for exercising cocreative capabilities. In
conjunction with the Higher Self within every person, the perspective of one's own inner ''master'' becomes our chosen pattern of
experience and growth.

Imagine the universe beautiful and just and perfect. Then be sure of one
thing: the Is has imagined it quite a bit better than you have.[23]

Crystals can be used in two basic ways for this purpose. One
method is to utilize them as a tool that connects consciousness more
clearly and strongly to the higher octaves of Light. Align personal
awareness with Divine Intelligence and then project the thought-

waves into and through the crystal, thus imprinting an energy pattern on multiple Light-dimensions. Continue this procedure for as long as necessary and repeat it on a daily basis. The other method is to program a suitable crystal with the desired energy pattern, then consciously connect this pattern to the higher octaves of Light through the medium of the crystal. Then place it in a relatively isolated environment where it will constantly transmit these patterns and thereby continually reinforce their manifestation process. It is also helpful with this technique to re-energize the programming on a regular basis.

You are never given a wish without also being given the power to make it true. You may have to work for it, however.[23]

Long-Distance Healing

Since quartz acts as an interdimensional connector, it is extremely well suited for the projection of healing energy from one location to another. On other dimensional planes, time and space do not exist, and physical distances are neutralized, one point never being apart from another point. The crystal, from this perspective, can be envisioned as a archetypal *axis mundi,* or Cosmic Tree, than spans the multidimensional realms as a central axis in which and through which these planes can be connected. Let us explore various applications of this principle.

In many techniques of long-distance healing, a "witness" of the healing recipient is used as a focal point through which a stronger energetic connection is made. The main idea of a witness is to have a vibrational representation of an individual, and such things as hair, saliva, and photographs have been used for this purpose. The witness is placed in direct energetic contact with the healing energies that are being transmitted. It then serves to clarify and amplify the vibrational connection to the recipient. Due to the nature of the witness' function, quartz will also perform these roles exceptionally well. By having the recipients program their personal vibrations into a crystal, these patterns are recorded and maintained within the DNA latticework. And as an interdimensional connector, it will provide even greater effectiveness as a transmissional link from one location to another. Before using a witness or applying any long-distance healing techniques, though, it is necessary to have the individual's permission, and thus the cosmic laws of Divine Order are fulfilled.

Dr. Benoytosh Bhattacharya, a noted spiritual scientist and author, has stimulated various gems to emit their characteristic frequencies and applied these emanations for long-distance healing.

A silver disc set with the desired gems may be prepared. The size may be three to four inches in diameter. This disc may be fitted to a small electric motor, and switched into action. As the motor whirls with a speed of say 1300 to 1400 RPM the gems yield their color. Any photograph of a diseased or healthy person kept before the radiating motor will at once receive the vibrations.

The cosmic colors can also be broadcast to either the healthy or the diseased person by vibrating the gems at very high frequency. This can be done via the Vibrator which vibrates at the rate of 3000 vibrations per minute.[24].

Another way to employ these two basic ideas is to use them with crystals programmed with various colors, tones, healing energies and other desired frequencies.

A teletherapy chamber may be built for both long-distance healing and as an adjunct to therapy sessions done in close proximity. One form of teletherapy chamber is shown in Figure 15. It basically consists of a $12'' \times 12''$-base pyramid set on top of a standard $12'' \times 12''$ square mirror. Other sizes of pyramids and mirrors are suitable, though it is optimal to have them identical in measurements at their juncture areas. Inside, place a basic diagram that shows the outline of a human body and chakra system. Then put crystals programmed to heal specific body areas or chakras on the corresponding section of the diagram. Best results will come about by focusing on one or two major focal regions at a time. Further, in order to key this energy field to the recipient, place the witness, preferably a crystal, on the third eye chakra area of the diagram. Better results will accrue if the collective energy field is strengthened. This can be accomplished by making gridwork systems both around the pyramid-mirror construct and surrounding the diagram inside. Crystals attached to the pyramid at the apex and other

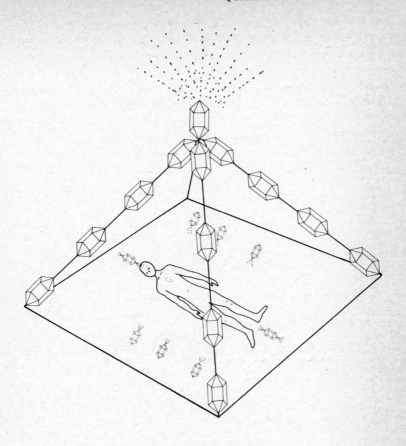

Figure 15: Teletherapy Chamber I

primary energy regions will also add to this amplification. Additionally, the placement of mandalas and sacred geometrical forms underneath the diagram that are appropriate for the individual is another means of magnifying the healing process.

Another example of a teletherapy chamber is shown in Figure 16. Two latticework configurations are constructed in either a dodecahedral

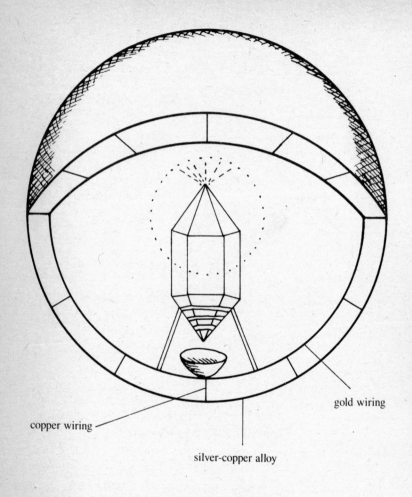

gold wiring

copper wiring

silver-copper alloy

Figure 16: Teletherapy Chamber II

or icosahedral geometry. Both levels are made of small-diameter copper, silver, or gold rods that are malleable enough to shape into the desired arrangement. Optimally, the outer level is silver, the inner level is gold, and copper connects the two together at each corresponding vertex so that a parallel conformity is created. Within the inner latticework, a double-termination crystal is held in place by gold supports and serves as the primary activator of the entire energy field. Directly underneath, a cuplike holder is made to hold the witness and crystals programmed for specific healing purposes. The entire chamber acts as a holistic amplification and transmitting device for the projection of healing energies that are encoded in the crystals retained by the cuplike holder. The energy patterns sent from this device can be augmented by additional energy input such as focused thought-projection or a surrounding gridwork system. Use this chamber with discretion, as it has potentially powerful effects.

Cooperating with the Crystal Devic Kingdom

As co-workers within the Divine Order, the various devic and elemental realms play an important role in maintaining all aspects of the natural world—the animal, plant, and mineral kingdoms. For many centuries these beings have been relatively restricted to a few remote regions around the world due to the great natural imbalances that exist. It is possible, though, to re-establish a harmonious and mutually beneficial relationship under suitable circumstances. Primarily, it is of the utmost importance to create and maintain a balanced and uplifting environment, for these beings cannot exist in the midst of disorder and disharmony. To invite them to live in close proximity, create a small "home" or sanctuary that will be their private and undisturbed space. It can be inside or outside, and it is beneficial to have "treasures" of nature in this place—plants, rocks, crystals, shells, fresh water, and so on. Prepare a devic (2) or an open-ended (16) crystal to be their primary home by clearing, cleansing, charging, activating, and programming it. During the programming process, visualize a clear, Light-filled space in the crystal with beautiful natural surroundings. Once all is ready, attune to the higher octaves of Light and consciously invite the crystal devas to live at this location and to work in harmony with you. It is helpful to state that all disharmony has been cleared away and a radiant home awaits them if they so desire it. Continue this process daily until a response occurs. The same procedure can be employed for all types of devas and elementals. Once some crystal devas are living in their new abode, they can be asked to assist in any number or tasks related to crystals—helping to gain new crystal knowledge, charging, activating, clearing, cleansing, and programming. Their direct assistance helps keep the crystals in optimal working condition and facilitates their higher-octave applications. In appearance, most of the crystal devas are 3–6 inches in height and look to be almost transparent, with glitters of Light emanating from the edges of their auras. They might be seen darting about in one's peripheral vision or more directly for those with auric sight. Working with these and other types of devas and elementals can be an enriching and edifying task toward gaining greater understanding of crystals and re-establishing a harmonious connection with this whole kingdom of Light-beings.

Miscellaneous Crystal Applications

1. Small crystals taped to the forehead or others of suitable size placed under a pillow during sleep enhance the clarity and intensity of dream states for many people. Much learning occurs during this time and crystals facilitate greater recall and integration of energy patterns and knowledge on all levels of the auric system.
2. Crushed quartz mixed in soil will noticeably invigorate the overall growth and health of plants. Also beneficial is to place a crystal directly adjacent to a plant with the point upward.
3. The facets and sides of crystals can be inscribed with spiritual symbols, sacred geometrical patterns, and mandalas in order to magnify the inherent programming and for amplifed attunement to each individual's unique harmonic vibrations. This effect can be augmented by packing gold within the inscriptions. When there is a harmonic resonance between the crystal's programming, the inscriptions, and person's vibratory patterns, the result is a very potent, activated tool.

4. Crushed quartz can be used in mortar in order to raise the general vibratory level of an entire building.
5. For use as a pendulum, quartz is the best medium for most accurately dowsing in a wide variety of situations and purposes.
6. As a focal point for extrasensory enhancement, the crystal ball made of quartz is the most effective tool. Quartz is the quintessential window of Light and no other earthly substance can serve this purpose as well.

True crystal gazing has been defined as the science of inhibiting normal outward consciousness by intense concentration on a polished crystal. When the five senses are thus drastically subdued, the psychic receptors can function without interference. Exactly why this alteration of consciousness works so well with crystal is not precisely understood. Many scientists and psychologists believe there is an energy interchange between certain portions of the brain and crystal. Thought waves as energy are very similar to radio waves. It is believed the crystal mass acts as a filtering antenna and amplifying reflector to the psychic receptor centers. Waves of energy from the brain trigger the crystal into activity which in return stimulates the sleeping psychic centers to awaken and function.[25]

7. Meditation done in direct outdoor sunlight with a crystal over the third-eye center facilitates the unfolding of all aspects of inner vision.
8. Placing crystals on windowsills with the points toward the inside of the house will help to draw increased energy into the entire room. Also, by putting crystals at various harmonic locations within a room, the whole area is vibrationally uplifted.
9. Research has shown that by applying the left hand to the third-eye area, ESP abilities are increased and stress is relieved.[26] By using this principle in conjunction with a crystal, the effect is amplified.
10. Pyramids and crystals blend together synergistically. By placing crystals at various key energy zones of the pyramidal form, the overall energies can be dramatically magnified. The apex, four corners, King's Chamber, Queen's Chamber, and the exact middle of the base are optimal regions where crystals can be hung with wire or glued in place (white glue serves

well). The construction of gridwork systems around and within the pyramid is a good idea with which to work. Small, thin double terminations strung in place wth wire at the phi (1:1.618 . . .) nodal points along the pyramidal sides are also excellent for energy activation.

The Relation Between Size and Power

As a general rule, the larger a crystal is, the more power it has due to increased volumetric capacity to process greater amounts of energy in a given time span. This is not always the case, though, as there are a number of other factors to consider. The first is the degree of activation. The process of activating a crystal is analogous to switching a multiwattage light bulb from 50 watts to 100 watts, or 100 watts to 150 watts. Dormant energy pathways are opened up in an activated crystal, making it "shine" with increased "wattage." Therefore, a smaller crystal that has a higher degree of activation could very well be more powerful than a larger crystal with a low activation quotient. Generally, though, given two crystals with the same activation quotient, the larger one will be more powerful in direct relationship to the difference in total volume. The second factor concerns the degree of clarity. Crystals with greater clarity are usually more potent than those that are murky and cloudy throughout the entire structure. Arkansas crystals and Herkimer "diamonds" from New York are two of the better-known sources of clear quartz. Many crystals have various inclusions (other elements within the crystalline structure) but still have a basic clarity around these additional substances, and therefore retain their dynamicism. The third factor concerns the greater inherent potency of the various categories of crystals in relationship to one another. Power-rods (1) and healing crystals (5), for example, are molecularly structured to process increased amounts of energy related to their functional purposes, versus the relatively lower energy requisites for, say, devic crystals (2) and library crystals (8). Basically, the structural programming of every category is related to a specified function that requires more or less raw energetic force to accomplish their respective roles; thus, each category differs in the parameters of its potential power level. This distinction, in addition to the factors discussed above, show that it is not uncommon to find smaller quartz specimens that are more powerful than larger ones. With additional increments of volume, however, crystals of greater size have increased statistical probability to be more inherently potent, hence the general rule of larger size signifying intensified force.

Left- vs. Right-Handed Crystals

All quartz crystals are either left-handed or right-handed, and nature affords approximately equal numbers of each. The difference is one of molecular structure—the left-handed crystal consists of a latticework of spirals rotating in a counterclockwise direction and the right-hand crystal consists of spirals in a clockwise direction. As energy enters the crystal, the plane of polarized vibration is rotated either to the left or to the right, depending on which direction the spirals revolve. This difference in the manner in which energy is processed through the crystalline structure creates a significant variance in the general characteristics of energy flow. The left-handed spiral tends to facilitate the absorption and gathering of energy into a crystal; the right-handed spiral tends to facilitate the projecting and disseminating of energy from the crystal. Therefore, in choosing a quartz for a specific function, it is good to relate the intended purpose with the nature of the crystal's overall energy flow. In healing, for example, a left-handed crystal is more conducive to absorbing negative energy patterns and a right-handed quartz is better suited to emanate positive healing vibrations. Some crystal practitioners disagree in various degrees with this perspective. And, as it is a relatively significant property, it is well to experiment further in this area on one's own to gain further experience from which to form conclusions.

With most crystals, it is very difficult to discern their handedness without the use of laboratory equipment. Relatively few have an "X" facet, a lozenge-shaped facet in addition to the normal six top facets that indicates by its positioning whether a crystal is left- or right-handed. For more detailed crystallographic information on this subject, a comprehensive mineralogical text will provide the knowledge.

Double-Termination Crystals

Crystals that have six-faceted terminations on both ends are called double terminations. These constitute a low percentage of total quartz specimens, as the great majority have one termination and an opposite unterminated base that attached to the matrix from which they grew. Double terminations, on the other hand, can grow totally in solution, unattached to the surrounding matrix rock, or they can be attached to the matrix of other crystals on their side, thus allowing two terminations to grow. As a group, they are some of the most powerful, complex, and useful crystals in existence. Relatively unimpeded in the growth process, they were allowed to manifest as a whole and perfect crystalline form. And it is in their property of wholeness that the key to their understanding lies. In single-terminated crystals, the primary energy emanations come forth from one six-faceted end while this effect occurs through both ends of double terminations. Further, the collective energetic activity is less hindered due to the lack of the opaque and more inert quartz commonly found at the base of single terminations. This activity is also more complex due to the internal refraction and reflection of energy within the dynamics of two terminations (vs. one). Because of this greater complexity their quality of wholeness produces, the holographic mode of functioning often has increased clarity and sophistication. Practically speaking, double terminations can be viewed as two-way avenues, with energy coming into and out of both ends. This is why, for example, an uncapped double-termination pendant will process auric energies both upward and downward while single terminations have only one main direction of emanation. In other applications, this property adds to the general effectiveness and efficiency, especially in such crystal categories as healing (5), vision (13), energy (4), transmitting (11), and modulatory (12). Overall, the unified energy field of these "perfect" crystals resonates strongly with the holistic nature of the Universal Mind, thus making them most valuable tools of Light.

Crystal Clusters

Clusters are defined as two or more crystals that are physically attached to one another by natural means. They range from clusters of two all the way to groupings of thousands. Each individual crystal within the grouping functions both as a distinct unit and as part of the whole. The interactions between all these conjoining units create a synergistic unified energy field. In unison, every grouping has an underlying base programming that designates its mode of functioning and optimal application. The distinct crystals within the cluster each have a subprogramming that relates to the base programming like a variation on a primary theme. For the most part, clusters are highly unique and therefore need to be evaluated individually in ascertaining their best usage. Consider the angular and energetic relationships between the crystals along with intuitive perception of the overall dynamics.

As previously mentioned in the gridwork systems section of this chapter, clusters emanate a more complex network of energy lines than single quartz specimens. Each crystal within a cluster projects a primary energy, and the intersection and blending between all of them forms a latticework pattern. Furthermore, these distinct crystals can be programmed separately within the harmonics of the underlying base programming. Various tones, colors, thought-frequencies, and so on may be encoded into specific individual crystals. Therefore, the energy latticework is able to be significantly modified to create a desired pattern to accomplish a particular purpose. In gridwork systems, these principles of application reach a pinnacle. By carefully and precisely programming each crystal within every gridwork cluster, a latticework can be manifested that will focus multiple energy lines on specific areas of the auric system simultaneously. In so doing, particular locations will receive exact mixtures of color, sound, and thought-frequencies. The entire network becomes a specialized field of wholeness and, in its higher octaves of use, has the capacity for instantaneous healing. On the other hand, single clusters can be applied by utilizing the same basic programming principles and will thereby serve to extend the spectral range of encoded energies that can be employed for particular purposes. Thus, clusters add a new dimension of complexity and sophistication to the realms of crystal energetics.

Colored Quartz

Quartz manifests in numerous varieties of coloration. Technically, these colors are created by impurities within the crystalline matrix and thereby modify the inherently clear crystal according to its corresponding hue. Amethyst, for example, is purple because of iron molecules incorporated into the quartz. It is the considered perspective of the authors that clear crystals are more powerful and versatile tools than those with coloration. Colored crystals are useful as specialized tools of a specific color frequency but their overall potency and holistic functioning is muted by the impurities. As previously discussed, a particular color frequency can be emphasized as the predominant programming of a clear crystal. This accentuated color functions within the holistic dynamics of the total spectrum of crystal energy interactions. The impurities of colored quartz, on the other hand, have the distinct property of narrowing the range of operational frequencies and impeding their full power. They still, however, retain many of the basic characteristics of quartz and therefore act in beneficial ways, especially within the frequency range of their coloration. This is to say that amethyst, for example, is useful as a tool of violet, but that a violet-programmed clear quartz will be more powerful and effective. This general perspective is not one that is shared by a significant percentage of crystal users and practitioners. The authors encourage each individual to do experiments that will help in demonstrating the difference between colored quartz and color-programmed quartz. For instance, take an amethyst and a violet-encoded crystal; do a number of awareness exercises with each and apply them in identical ways, noticing any variations in perceptions and results between the two. In this manner of open-minded experimentation, each person will be able to draw his or her own informed conclusions.

Presented below is a collection of accepted mineralogical facts regarding the major forms of colored crystals:

1. *Amethyst:*

   Chemical analyses of amethyst show it to be nearly pure SiO_2 but always containing some iron (less than 0.10 percent). Since the amount of iron increases with increasing depth of color it is assumed that this element is the coloring agent. Although the color is completely stable at ordinary temperatures, heating produces a remarkable change. If it is heated to 450°C the mineral becomes colorless; but if heated to 550°C it turns to a yellowish brown, the color of citrine.[27]

   It is also reported that heat treatment can turn amethyst into a deep reddish-yellow ("Rio Grande topaz") or pale green.[28]

2. *Citrine*: Its yellow to yellow-brown coloration is also caused by iron.[29]

3. *Rose quartz*: Its shades of light pink to deep rose-red are due to small amounts of titanium.[30]

4. *Smoky quartz*: This type of crystal has a color that varies in intensity from pale brown to nearly totally black.

   If a smoky quartz is heated at 450°C the "smoke" vanishes in a few minutes, leaving the crystal colorless, but unaffected in other ways. The color can be restored by irradiating the bleached crystal in a beam of X-rays. For this reason and because chemical analysis fails to detect any impurity not present in colorless quartz, many believe that the color of smoky quartz is the result of a natural irradiation.[31]

Natural vs. Synthetic Crystals

Natural quartz crystals have a level of sentience and intelligence that is not found in the artificially produced crystals that are created with current-day technology. The workings of the Universal Mind in conjunction with the devas, elementals, angels, and other kingdoms infuse life and consciousness into each crystal as it is formed in the bowels of the Earth over hundreds and thousands of years. The spiritual alchemy that occurs in this process does not happen in laboratory conditions as they exist today. The technological manufacturing of quartz and the many other kinds of crystalline substances is a very sophisticated science that creates crystals in a matter of days or weeks under controlled man-made conditions. The lack of uniting spiritual knowledge with scientific principles results in precise and predictable, but lifeless, crystals. One example of this is the lead crystals that adorn many stores and homes. Attractive though they are, these prismatic objects have little or no spiritual or healing applications. They are a manufactured combination of glass, which has a random molecular structure, and lead oxide, which helps to create the pleasing rainbows of color. Together, these elements are as a man-made ruby is to a natural ruby, a synthetic quartz to a natural quartz—dim reflections of holistic crystals formed through Divine Intelligence.

In the highly advanced civilizations of the past, man employed spiritual wisdom and cooperation with the devas, elementals, and so on, in conjunction with scientific knowledge to create sentient crystals. Rev. Dr. Frank Alper reports that some of them in these days were "apports," or crystals materialized from higher-dimensional planes. Highly evolved beings on these levels would crystallize the "universal energy mass" into the desired form and then transport it to the physical plane.[32] Aaron Abrahamsen has channeled information regarding an Atlantean "Laboratory of Life" where life-giving crystals were cocreated with music, light, chemical solutions, and finely tuned human consciousness.

. . . [C]rystals, life-giving stones. The production of these were then made by many methods. Much was done by music. For you see, even the very nuclei, even the very orbits within each crystalline structure is alive, they respond to music. They respond also to light, color. . . . It was a very high vibration going about because each person had spent time in raising the vibration each day. . . . For the music, even as it was playing to the crystals, was also heard by the humans, you see? And so the atmosphere was one of cooperation. In other words, here then is where they endeavored to cooperate with nature in finding the principles for growth. . . .[33]

As Divine Science evolves to a greater degree, we will once again find the alchemical means to blend Spirit with matter in order to manifest many varieties of living crystals, precision-made for multitudes of specific purposes, toward the mutual benefit of the kingdoms of man and minerals.

Inclusions

Quartz inclusions are substances other than those of the pure chemical formula of SiO_2 (silicon dioxide) that are included within the crystalline matrix. Due to the great abundance of quartz throughout the Earth's crust, the variety of inclusions is profuse and a complete course of study in and of itself. To be discussed here are those inclusions that are of primary significance to the realms of crystal applications presented in this text. Three elements are the most important in this regard—water, aluminum, and rutile. Quartz dissolves readily in water under high pressure and temperature, and during the growth process liquid droplets and gas bubbles adhere to the developing crystal faces and are subsequently covered up. This results in the veils and wisps of water and gas inclusions seen in so many crystals. In some cases they are so numerous that the entire quartz is milky or even opaque. When used for healing and self-transformation the water inclusions react differently to the incoming energies than the surrounding silicon dioxide. Primarily, the response of water inclusions is one of greater agitation than the quartz. This can be envisioned as tiny pockets of "boiling" water amidst the more evenly flowing crystal energies. The agitated energy from the water is transferred to the crystalline matrix, thus modifying the overall energy dynamics to a relatively subtle degree. The wisps and veils of water inclusion therefore influence the crystal interactions according to their patterns within the quartz. This is not to say that such inclusions necessarily make a crystal more powerful; rather, it is more a matter of emphasis of the water's patterns within the crystalline matrix. A wisp of enclosed water, then, will influence the crystal's overall energies according to the undulatory patterns of the wisp.

Aluminum is seen in quartz specimens as shiny "mirrors" occurring in many shapes, from undulating sheets to planar patterns to wisps and veils. It is differentiated from water and gas inclusions by its reflective quality. According to the aluminum's pattern, it will reflect crystal energies at precise angles, thus significantly modifying the overall energy dynamics. Again, this is a matter of modulation and not necessarily an increase of power. Energies being processed through a crystal will be reflected at precise angles by the aluminum inclusions, thus modifying the energies into precise vibratory patterns. This element also has the capacity to assist in the retention of programming codes. In some cases, these inclusions are "coating" and protecting already-existing codings of a higher order as found in archetype (7) and library (8) crystals.

And lastly, rutile is a form of crystal composed of titanium dioxide manifesting as very thin, elongated needles. This substance is similar in nature to silver and copper regarding its capacity to transfer and modulate energy. Generally, the patternings of rutile will code the crystal to process energy in precise ways. The rutiles form the primary pathways of energy modification and transference. In addition this element strengthens and transmutes the crystal energies to a relatively small but significant degree.

These three primary inclusions, then, serve essentially as secondary adjuncts and modifiers of crystal energy dynamics.

Natural vs. Man-Made Faceting

The question of whether crystals in their natural state are superior to those faceted by man (and vice versa) cannot be answered by a general rule but rather involves the discrimination of the status of each unique crystal. On the one hand, there are many that man cannot improve upon, for the imprint of the Universal Mind bears its mark of consummate craftsmanship. So, too, there are others that need to be faceted through the hand of man in order for their full potentialities to be activated. With proper knowledge and intuitive sensitivity, man can mold "raw" quartz into a more refined and precise tool. Just as the master artist "sees" the end-product in a block of marble or wood and reveals the inner essence already there, so also can man bring forth the inherent perfection and highest potentials of crystals. The most important factor in this regard is one of discrimination. First, man must be able to tell the difference between naturally perfected crystals and those that are in a relatively unrefined state. In addition, the process of faceting is a highly individual one, unique to each crystal. Inherent within every quartz is a programming, a set of configurational dictums, that sets the patterns of peak usage. This is in contradistinction to the practice of shaping quartz into standard faceting patterns. With applied insight into sacred geometry in conjunction with crystal energetics, each distinct crystal can be faceted into an optimal format. Furthermore, within the patterns of this format, secondary alterations can be made to attune the crystal's overall harmonic frequencies to those of a person's auric system. Personal crystals, for example, can be produced in this way, along with more specific applications, such as shaping a vision crystal (13) to match its inherent programming with an individual's third-eye frequencies. On the other hand, the faceting, shaping, or polishing of any crystal for aesthetic purposes alone are practices that downgrade and disrupt the natural energy flow. It should be emphasized that *any* alterations performed need to be done with great discernment and spiritual intention. So, the perfection of each crystal can be brought forth through the discriminating hand of man and can also be attuned to the singular harmonics of an individual's auric system. Thereby, as man facets crystals, he also facets his own crystalline self, revealing the Divine essence of both.

Thus concludes this chapter. Use it as a workbook to come back to again and again for deeper insight and new ideas. Notice as you do how these "sparks" of Light ignite the flame of Self-realization.

Chapter 6

CRYSTAL VISIONS

Images of Divine Science

Like the charting of a new star
the new awakening of humanity
only makes visible
a light that has been present all along
but was unseen
because we didn't know where to look.
—MARILYN FERGUSON, Ph.D.,
author of *Aquarian Conspiracy*

The dawning of a new era of consciousness growth brings with it new knowing, ancient knowing, and the Light of transformation that opens brilliant vistas, long forgotten and recently rekindled. The Light of crystals is one such key of remembering and catalyzing of Celestial Light on Earth. Let us recall the Lightbeings that we truly are, for nothing else is the truth other than the Light that we embody. The very Earth that we stand upon is changing; molecule by molecule it is being uplifted with increasing swiftness. Let us keep pace, continuing to be open to new ideas, even if this Light facilitates the painful release of a new-age-become-old into a New World of unlimited cosmic dimensions. The Light of the inner self beckons forth with increasing reverberations . . . great courage is needed in heeding this call, for it means nothing less than total surrender to the Higher Self within each and every one of us . . . to do so is to ride the lightning bolt to a higher destiny . . . a world of Light undreamed of. . . .

Visions, seed-thoughts, catalysts, ideas, and imaginings—this is the fabric of which this chapter is woven. Enjoy this voyage of past, present, and future . . . from technical detail to visionary realism. . . .

The science of harmony in music is, in these terms, practically identical with the science of symmetry in crystals. Indeed the crystals can now literally be seen to be the philosopher's stone, frozen music which presents to the eye . . . the dynamism of the molecules, atoms, particles, and standing waves of which they are composed. . . ."[1]

      —PROFESSOR G. C. AMSTUTZ, director of the Mineralogical and
        Petrographic Institute of the University of Heidelberg

*

At the Zeileis Clinic in Gallspach, Austria, there is a treatment room consisting totally of precious stones set in certain arrangements behind glass. Patients walk between the opposite rows of gems, once up and once back, either every day or every other day according to the nature of their complaint. These treatments have proven to be very effective.[2]

*

Physicist Arnold Zachow has stated that if the capstone of the Pyramid of Giza were made of crystalline copper sheeting containing a multifaceted group of crystals, then it could function as a gigantic capacitor or accumulator.[3]

*

Genetics, with its research into DNA and RNA, has explained much, but it may not be the entire explanation. DNA may actually be a harmonic wave guide for holographic information being imprinted from the subtler level existing in higher velocity harmonics. . . . This holographic imprinting of the subtle body on the physical body occurs, no doubt using the DNA as a wave guide or physical molecular resonator to tune in these holographic imprints.[4]

*

The crystal is bestowed by God so that the mind can receive His command directly as in the days of the first Adamic creation when the jewel body of Light was a physical reality.[5]

*

Baron Karl von Reichenback, one of the foremost spiritual scientists of the nineteenth century, found "odic force" emanating from crystals in his experiments. He reports:

. . . [T]he whole of the crystal glowed through and through with a delicate light, and that over the pointed end there was a luminosity, blue in color, going upwards in a continually waving motion, scintillating now and then, in the form of a tulip losing itself above in a fine vapor. When I reversed the crystal she saw over the blunt end a dull reddish-yellow haze arising.[6]

*

Wally Richardson and Lenora Huett, in *Spiritual Value of Gem Stones*, provide information regarding a large Atlantean prism used as a power station.

. . . [I]t was used in such a way as to utilize the rays of the sun and the atmospheric conditions of the universe, so that they were brought into play on this planet. This energy was brought into this planet, broken up and re-arranged in such a way as to be used for power. It would draw this energy in and send it to a generator or a piece of machinery of comparable nature and store it. It was able to attract from outer space areas, the strong vibrations that are necessary to cause energy and power.[7]

*

Perhaps one day crystals will be encoded with holographic sequences of interdimensional realities and, when projected around the participants, will actually facilitate a direct transfer of consciousness to these dimensional planes.

The video screen was immediately filled with ever-expanding and evolving geometric patterns. The room was filled with soothing resonant sounds that seemed to cause my whole mind and body to resonate in similarly evolving and enlarging patterns. . . . I found myself flowing on a gentle river of multiple sensations until I seemed to enter an infinite ocean of unspeakable unity, oneness, and balance accompanied by the most soul-satisfying feeling of harmony imaginable.[8]

*

Crystal lattices have preferred axes or geometrical directions of electrical, magnetic and sonic conductivity. These properties can be used to set up highly coherent wave guides for standing wave electromagnetic fields. Properly used, these properties can also bring about conditions of superconductivity and zero light absorption in a crystal.[9]

*

Many of the monolithic stone circles around the world, like Stonehenge, have a high percentage of quartz within the stones themselves.

The piezoelectric properties of quartz and its ability to convert mechanical deformation (compression) into a static charge arise because the open structure of the helical array has an innate compressibility. . . . The structure of quartz possibly converts earth currents. If quartz is linked to underground water-courses, a conversion from hydrostatic pressure into static electricity may occur. The periodicity of the force observed could be a reflection of the original energy variation transformed by the quartz. . . . Therefore it's possible that the precise geometry of many stone circles, the exact configuration of hillforts, mounds, and tumps constructed by the ancients, were aimed at retaining this elusive force, until such time as it could be discharged.[18]

*

There may be ways of infusing various sound frequencies into specific crystals that, when placed together, would work harmonically to produce visions of celestial worlds. These special groupings would be "keys" to conscious coparticipation in other-dimensional realms.

*

Recall in the movie *Superman* the glowing green crystal that "called" to Clark Kent and how, when he threw it into the North Pole ice, it catalyzed the manifestation of the Fortress of Solitude, itself totally crystalline in nature. Perhaps there are such "seed-crystals" in existence today that will perform a similar function in facilitating a new world era.

*

The priests knew only too well that the sky rippled with electric currents, the air itself radiated heat waves, and that power without wires was theirs. They could call on the atmosphere for everything they needed.

They knew the code of the crystal.

They had trained others to amplify electricity by storing energy in special crystals. They had shown that crystals could generate more energy than they received. And this was not all—they had also taught others to harness the Sun's rays through crystals and store the energy in power stations built under the earth—to concentrate light waves into fine laser beams for building and reaching long-distance goals.[11]

*

IBM is currently working on developing a computer storage technology employing crystals and lasers. The lasers are used to create extremely small, micron-size spots inside the crystal at precise locations. Information is stored as a pattern of such spots according to both spatial coordinates and different color frequencies of the laser beam. Scientists are projecting that such a system will eventually be able to store the equivalent of all the books in the Library of Congress in a space about the size of a refrigerator.[13]

*

J. J. Hurtak writes of ancient scriptures containing the wisdom and technological expertise of highly advanced civilizations, many of which are encoded in quartz.

. . . [T]he quartz crystal texts which illustrate the piezoelectric effect. This activity shows how crystals can be used as (the primal energy) charge for the necessary "stimulation," causing the consciousness to enter and leave the body.[13]

*

In *Project: World Evacuation* by Tuella, crystals are referred to in relationship to the "Galactic Confederation."

There will be an identifying crystal of certain color for each, which immediately indicates the group to which that person is assigned, as well as the Sector Commander. This central stone will also be the crystal that is in attunement with the body vibrations of the one who who wears it and who is in direct contact with his Commander craft. The device will also have a factor incorporated into its design which will serve as levitating or traveling device for any emergency, as well as another built-in deposit of crystalline energy functioning as the means of producing invisibility as needed in times of danger.[14]

*

Royal Raymond Rife has invented a way of using circular, wedge-shaped quartz crystal prisms to polarize Light in such a way as to produce visibility of Light-spectrums beyond the range of the electron microscope.

In the "heterodyning effect" light from two vibrational frequencies interplay to establish two new frequencies. This medium of transposing light allows the Rife instrument to re-create bands of light running into the several higher, invisible octaves of the ultraviolet end of the scale. Thus Rife's microscope joins ultraviolet beams with other oscillations to manifest light in the eye of the viewer, otherwise lying beyond the realm of visibility.[15]

*

Spinning crystals can create very powerful energy fields in relationship to their overall harmonics, rate of spin, and energy projected into their structure. The infusion of lasers, particle beams, crystal-modulated thought-frequencies, and other energies into these rotating crystals would manifest a 360-degree field of a specified vibratory quality.

*

It is a scientifically verified fact that the combination of carbon and oxygen in biological systems can transmute into silicon. The chemical formula for this reaction is $C_{12} + O_{16}$ yields Si_{28}. Also, carbon plus silicon can transmute into calcium—$C_{12} + Si_{28}$ yields Ca_{40}.[16]

*

Fire crystals are devices which entrain vibrations moving at higher harmonics of the speed of light to electromagnetic standing wave fields. Through resonant circuitry connected with the crystals which draw power out of the crystals, the crystals can also be modulated to some extent in their electromagnetic frequencies and amplitudes. The modulation is harmonically passed on through the etheric fields or higher velocity fields that the electromagnetic field in the crystal is harmonically entrained with. These modulations can be picked up by other crystals tuned to the same frequency and these modulations are harmonically transferred to the electromagnetic fields of the receiving crystal. Thus, the crystals could be used for communication as well as power generating devices.[17]

*

Crushed quartz combined with other minerals and programmed crystals may be used as an activating "fertilizer" for creating new strains of vegetables, grains, and fruits.

*

Music, particularly ultrasonic music in the presence of heat, has been found capable of changing the chemical structure and the strength of crystals by spreading imperfections at grain boundaries in the lattice.[18]

*

Marcel Vogel has performed a number of experiments concerning the measurement of energy emanating from crystals. In one experiment using his specialized technique of projecting crystal energy, a photomultiplier tube indicated that a definite amount of energy was emitted accompanying a forced exhalation. In another experiment with a crystal connected to a voltmeter, it was found that by rubbing the crystal, the device indicated a definite current of energy.[19]

*

Crystals can be used to store genes of finer traits, acting as a component in enlightened genetic engineering. There may already be such crystals in existence, storing the work of previous civilizations.

*

Scientist Richard L. Clark, Ph.D., in an article entitled "Systems Engineering: ELF Antigravity Theory," reports on the possibility of employing extremely low frequencies (ELF) for antigravity applications.

The Earth is a natural generator system as a giant crystalline structure. By proper tuning and construction the UFOs are propelled and navigate on the Earth Grid. . . . Once you have oriented enough of the atoms in the substance to cross zero weight, the Earth will *push* the mass away—antigravity drive. . . . Piezoelectric crystal signal generators must have been Atlantean levitation devices, based on the same principal.

*

Scientists now studying thought-photography believe a crystal or systems of crystals can be a clue. "Crystals," they say, "are subject to mind-brain energy patterns, and if grown to become specific geometric shapes the prisms could likely be tuned to the mental frequency range of certain individuals," according to one spokesman. These far-seeing scientists foresee sensitive instruments containing numerous bands responsive to a multitude of thought patterns passing through various crystals.[20]

*

If the harmonic resonant frequency of certain crystals were duplicated by sonic frequencies and projected into the crystal, this coupling of energies would serve to activate great numbers of soft electrons within the crystalline structure. This would release great quantities of stored energy that could be regulated by the intensity of the sound and by periodically oscillating it between frequencies of phase entrainment and out-of-phase vibrations.

. . . [I]t seems appropriate to cite the increasing evidence that, in magnetically ordered crystals, the spins of the atoms periodically do something that could be called a flip, reversing their direction and polarity, just as happens much more slowly to the magnetic polarity of the Earth, the sun and stars and probably the galaxies. And this change actually advances from atom to atom like a row of falling dominoes in a microprogression physicists call a spin wave that sweeps through the material like a swell on the ocean. Indeed it is a vital factor in the melodic reality behind the wave nature of all matter.[21]

*

General Electric's research and development center has developed a new type of optical fiber made of quartz capable of transmitting very high-intensity laser beams sufficient for cutting and drilling metals. This is hundreds of times more intense than the Light-beams projected in fiber-optic communications. In factory use, for example, these quartz fibers will run from a single laser to multiple stations and will be much easier to employ than the more cumbersome mirrors and prisms currently used to direct laser beams.[22]

*

Try to image the waves in a crystal as an imploding tornado of light in a greenhouse. . . . The greenhouse windows, crystal surface facets are highly polished and in careful geometric arrangement. They determine the critical angles and corridors (of "sunlight"), such that energy entrance is permitted only at the angles which will focus directly at the center. Once inside bouncing through the center, all the light is reflected back to the center: a "greenhouse effect." The central focus has the function of developing a self-maintaining vortex of congruent field levels, folding through itself and reflecting from the other side. This continuous feedback upon itself, at the center, has the function of reinforcing the flow intensity, until *it penetrates to another flow level*. ("Flow" being fairly synonymous with frequency and energy, here.) What only then can finally pass right through the greenhouse windows is the higher harmonic, higher coherent, higher "dimension," wave field.[23]

*

Recall the movie *Dark Crystal* in which the gigantic focal crystal is the power source for the civilization, and the replacement of a displaced piece, or shard, catalyzes an incredible transformation of consciousness and matter into a higher, celestial level. Perhaps there is a metaphorical insight to be learned from this that applies to today.

*

Lama Sing has channeled information concerning Atlantean crystal science:

It is known that a beam of light directed intensely and focused specifically on a certain series of facets in a gem will, when it exists from the reflective plane of the gem, be amplified rather than diminished. And further, that the spectrum of the energies would be segmented so as to be more usable. . . . The Atlanteans used the spectrum of this energy for specific purposes, much as you use petroleum in terms of its various spectrum limitations for specific purposes. They used certain divisions of the energy for knowledge or increasement of substance. Other phases of the spectrum for disassembling molecule structures, and yet other combination of these strata for building, assembling molecular chains . . . or producing matter, transmutation of matter and that sort.[24]

*

The RCA Corporation has reported the development of a method of storing photographs, drawings, maps, statistics, and computer data in a crystal smaller than a sugar cube. Still in its research stage, it uses lasers to permanently implant images inside a specially developed crystal. The images are then retrieved by rotating the crystal at different angles in a laser beam.[25]

*

The ancient Egyptians well understood, first of all, that certain materials give off certain specific energies. For example, they utilized Aswan granite in many key locations within their Temples and Pyramids, because of its high crystalline content, which under pressure can create a piezoelectric field. The King's Chamber in the Great Pyramid is made entirely of Aswan granite, and with nearly three hundred feet of limestone pressing down on it from above, the Chamber generates a field that is detectable with a magnetometer and other electrical sensing equipment.[26]

*

Crystals are to be used as cyberg devices to amplify and filter communication signals.

They are used by the Higher Evolution as fundamental building blocks to set up a measurable grid of a larger harmonic system which allows for different combinations of wave structures to unite and form myriads of gravitational wave combinations which, in turn, react with one another to transmit thought-forms to physical planetary realities.

*

Angles of the prismatic cut established ratios and proportions of energy and its release and use. How the angles of multiple crystals are put together is highly important, for each one can be used as part of a whole system for creating, manifesting, generating, or amplifying various energies.

*

The alchemy of Sound may be further instanced in the response of minerals to the tonic effect of sound waves, and other octaves of vibrations. This is demonstrable in the fact that "blemishes" may be removed from jewels, and their luster improved by immersing them in a bath of sound reverberating their "key-note."[28]

*

Westinghouse scientists have developed a crystal made of thallium arsenic selenide that can double a laser beam's frequency; that is, if the beam enters the crystal as infrared, it emerges from the other side as green. Such a crystal can be connected to a transducer, which converts electric signals into mechanical vibrations. As the electrical vibrations going into the crystal change, it compresses or expands correspondingly, and thus changes the velocity of the light moving through it. By adjusting the current to the transducer, the crystal can be electronically tuned to create specific wavelengths without any need for lens changes. This vastly expands the versatility of devices incorporating this type of crystal, as the necessity for lens changes to create different wavelengths of energy are quite cumbersome.[29]

*

In the functioning of the physical body, the element of silicon is the "electric" substance that helps ensure the proper transmission of brain messages to the rest of the body. It also plays a role in the workings of the nervous system, glandular systems, hair, skin, and nails. It is possible that a certain percentage of silicon in the body is needed to facilitate superconscious, conscious, and subconscious communications with the higher octaves of Light.

*

A spiritual scientist, Louis Acker, reports:

UFO contactees that I have spoken to who claim to have been inside UFOs state the the propulsion systems for such spacecraft are based on the use of crystals. . . . By producing directional vectors in the imploding higher velocity harmonic vortexes of the crystal, the frictional drag that this imploding field produces with the electromagnetic standing wave pattern of the crystal pulls the crystal and its associated spacecraft through space. It has been further stated by these sources that the crystal is directionally oriented facing the largest gravitational mass in the vicinity toward which the craft is moving, thus aligning its field with the etheric flow pattern that exists around large gravitational masses such as a planet, star, etc.[30]

*

It may be possible to synthetically grow crystals according to desired specifications through the use of sonics, laser beams, holograms, and focused pyramidal energies.

*

Bjorn Ortenheim, a highly acclaimed Swedish scientist, reports that many of his innovative inventions have been the direct result of guidance from higher-dimensional planes. He has stated that the original crystal on top of the Great Pyramid was a large solar spectrum crystal.

In its original shape and site on the Great Pyramid, the crystal was separating the visible colors from the sunbeams and the invisible power colors from the UMF [Unified Magnetic Field]. . . . These separated colors were reflected into the two-chamber system in the pyramid, where the various powers of these colors were focused in huge lenses that were moved forward and backward in the great gallery.[31]

*

Some of the crystals were shaped in a form like an inverted pyramid, with a rounded or bell bottom. These crystals were made with either four or six sides. They were utilized in an inverted position, with the point down. The energy entered these crystals through the bell surface, which was now on the top and was multifaceted to allow for the greatest concentration of energy to flow into the crystal. This energy was then concentrated and flowed down to the point where it was dispersed with pinpoint accuracy and intensity for what you would refer to as surgery.[32]

*

Crystals may function as tools for infusing the power of Light into fluid form, thus making liquid Light a reality.

*

The placing of the crystal pyramidal energy cap over the crown chakra of an evolving humanity demonstrates how the consciousness of Man can be attached to other space-time dimensions so as to experience the face forms of the Lords of Light, who will reconstruct this present biochemical program to be in tune with the changing electromagnetic frequency.[33]

*

Mirrors will be instrumental in the decoding of numerous archetype and library crystals. The mirrors will be placed around the crystal at precise angles and then the reflections are photographed from a circle of angles.

*

Harmonics are frequencies that are integral multiples of an original frequency. Scientists at the University of Michigan have produced laser harmonics by focusing a 6943-Angstrom red beam from a ruby laser into a block of quartz. Coming out the other side was a blue beam of wavelength 3472 Angstroms, the second harmonic (a doubling of the original frequency). This blue beam was very weak in beginning experiments, but later its intensity was as much as 20 percent of the original red beam.[34]

With lower-octave Light, great intensities of energy are required in order to generate multiple harmonics through quartz. In the future, scientists will find that the insulative properties of quartz crystal are considerably less on the higher octaves of Light, and therefore the creation of harmonics is highly energy efficient. Also, with increased activation of a given crystal, its harmonic efficiency is magnified correspondingly.

*

. . . [S]hips—cylindrical craft that sailed through the air and water alike, their engines guided by crystal gyroscopes. . . .[35]

*

The crystal, when flawlessly grown in the laboratory and faceted to exact geometrical proportions and critical dimensions, is capable of setting up such coherent electromagnetic standing wave fields by coherently harmonically phase locking all the different electromagnetic, sonic and higher dimensional vibrations that can occur in a crystal in a vector equilibrium standing wave pattern. When a high degree of electromagnetic standing wave coherency is generated in the crystal, it can harmonically match modes with higher velocity harmonics and set up a high conductivity wave guide vortex for these higher velocity harmonics, thus establishing an imploding vortex of vibrations in the higher velocity harmonics which continuously harmonically pumps the electromagnetic field in the crystal, thus becoming a source of energy.[36]

*

Then she explained how cosmic radiation was combined with the forces created by the movement of the earth. These were captured, reactivated, reflected, and amplified by a crystal, then broadcast, creating a central power source. Power was obtained through electro-acoustical tuning to this source.[37]

*

The basic texture of research consists of dreams into which the threads of reasoning, measurement and calculation are woven. —ALBERT SZENT-GYORGYI, M.D., Ph.D.

A man who has lost his sense of wonder is as a man dead. Logic can take you from A to B, but imagination encircles the world. —ALBERT EINSTEIN

. . . [F]or those who are awake there is one common Kosmos, but to those who sleep each turns aside into his own world. —HERACLITUS

Chapter 7

CRYSTAL MEDITATIONS

Multifaceted Inner Explorations

The meditations presented in this chapter are designed to expand awareness of the crystalline nature of creation. As inner voyages into the multifaceted aspects of manifestation, they will help open the windows of perception into the higher octaves of Light. Try recording them on cassette tapes and using them repeatedly; this is an optimal way of progressively gaining greater insight and depth of "crystal consciousness." Enjoy your journeys into Crystal-Light!

Sensing the Crystal Meditation

For this meditation, you should choose a very special crystal— one you feel really comfortable with. It may not be your most beautiful crystal but will certainly be one of your favorites.

After you put your crystal in between both hands, assume a relaxing meditative position . . . and let go of stress completely . . . close your eyes . . . relax . . . get into the flow of the universe . . . spend a few minutes just relaxing and letting go of all worldly thoughts and feelings. Then, slowly begin to focus your attention to your crystal . . . feel its energy and love . . . as it reflects that inner comfort of your being . . . enjoy this peaceful feeling for awhile. Then very slowly let your awareness spiral down into the crystal . . . keep your eyes closed and feel how gently you glide . . . down into the center of your crystal . . . deeper and deeper . . . until you feel you can no longer move. You are at the core of your crystal now . . . do not open your eyes yet . . . relax . . . begin to experience with your consciousness exactly what a crystal feels like. Is it cool or warm . . . is it dry or damp . . . is it smooth or rough? Feel it . . . reach out and touch it . . . experience it completely with your touch. Then be still once more . . . gradually tune in to any sounds your crystal is making. Can you hear it . . . very faintly at first . . . listen closely to the tone . . . to the pitch . . . to the resonating frequencies of harmony . . . enjoy the singing . . . relax and enjoy. And as the sounds diminish . . . take a few slow, deep breaths of crystalline energy through the nostrils . . . smell your crystal . . . take another breath and smell the crystal again. Is it an aroma you're familiar with, or is it a new sensation? Enjoy the cleanness . . . the purity. Open your mouth slightly and let the taste of your crystal enter slowly. Is it like water . . . or is it of even higher vibration? Feel the smoothness in your mouth . . . taste the energy . . . experience it totally. Relax and experience . . . you are safe within your crystal . . . totally relaxed and calm and safe. Feel this as you gently open your eyes . . . open your eyes to see your crystal . . . the bright White Light glowing and glittering all about you. View the mirrors and symbols and images unique to this crystal . . . see the veins of energy shooting all around you . . . gaze on the rainbows that fly through the clear, shiny surfaces . . . look at the facets . . . the windows of your crystals as they intensify the energy with their angles . . . open your eyes to splendor before unseen. Then become aware of the taste again . . . then the aroma . . . then the sounds and singing . . . and the touch of the crystal. Your senses are alive for the first time as you experience your crystal . . . continue this marvelous encompassing experience for as long as you wish.

When you are ready to bring this back with you to your own consciousness on the physical realm . . . count to three very slowly and feel yourself spiraling out of the crystal and back into your body . . . back into the physical plane, but bringing with you your now activated and fully awakened senses . . . to experience the world always with a sparkling crystal awareness.

Seed Crystal Meditation

For this meditation, you will either need to lay down and place a crystal on your heart center or sit with a crystal pendant suspended on the heart center.

After becoming comfortable and relaxed . . . close your eyes and take a few slow, deep breaths . . . and relax . . . totally relax . . . let yourself melt into the flow of Light that constantly surrounds you. After a few moments, become aware of the vibrations emanating from the crystal on your heart center . . . in your mind, see it glowing with bright White Light . . . see this small focal point of Light as your personal seed-crystal . . . waiting to beam out its Light throughout the universe . . . making your body, your being, a brilliant crystal also. As you continue to concentrate on your seed crystal . . . see it growing brighter and brighter . . . the Light is so pure, so white. The crystal begins to vibrate with cosmic energy . . . and as the vibration increases, the crystal shoots a white laser Light beam down the body . . . activating and energizing the lower chakras of the body. Feel the Light . . . experience it in each center. Then focus back to your seed-crystal . . . as it vibrates, again it shoots a bright white laser beam into the chakras of the body . . . filling them with the same pure energy that fills the lower chakras. Be aware of the intensity of the Light as it permeates the very core of your existence . . . then be aware of your seed-crystal. The vibrations have increased . . . more and more they increase again . . . until the crystal begins to spin . . . slowly at first . . . spinning slowly . . . and as the crystal energy generates, the crystal spins more quickly now . . . more quickly. With the spinning Light of the crystal, the beams of Light that shoot into the upper and lower chakras begin to spin also . . . slowly at first and then quickly . . . in perfect synchronization, until the spinning of the seed-crystal is weaving a Light energy field in a perfect circle around the body. An intricate mandala of Light surrounds the body now . . . spinning and weaving, the Light moves so quickly that the outer rim of the Light mandala begins to lift into the air while the center maintains its attachment to your seed-crystal. Higher and higher the rim of the circle lifts . . . forming a funnel of Light into the heart center. As the speed increases even more, the funnel spirals down into the heart chakra . . . and as it hits the seed-crystal . . . an explosion of White Light fills your auric field and drifts over your body in waves of glittering crystal energy . . . leaving your body pure and clear . . . as a crystal. Yes, you are a crystal . . . a seed-crystal of the universe . . . feel yourself glowing and shining . . . emanating bright, white crystal Light. Enjoy this for a few minutes and as you bring your consciousness back to the seed-crystal on your heart center . . . you realize that you and the seed-crystal are one. You *are* the crystal . . . and as you fully awaken, the experience is now a part of you . . . you are a crystal!

Crystal Palace Meditation

This meditation will take you to a place you've always wanted to go . . . your own crystal palace . . . a place to let your being totally relax . . . a place of immense love and warmth and caring . . . your home. Lay down and put your crystal on your third-eye area . . . take a few slow, deep breaths and relax your entire body . . . experience the relaxation for a few minutes . . . feel the energy around you flow calmly . . . relax and let go of the body . . . let go of the body completely. Allow your consciousness to flow slowly up to the third-eye center . . . and into the awaiting crystal. Once in the crystal, you feel yourself being transported through the cosmos . . . you feel light and free . . . full of pure, crystal energy. Ahead of you, you gaze at a beautiful crystal city . . . glimmering with White Light filled with glitters of silver and gold . . . you have never seen such a beautiful place. As you get closer to the crystal city . . . you see that each building is made of clear, shining crystal . . . each is lit with bright energy from within. As you walk through the city, you see the tall, irregular angles forming brilliant arches in the sky . . . the ground below you is made of millions of small diamondlike crystals . . . all sparkling in the Light. You wander down roads and walkways . . . this section of the city is beginning to look very familiar . . . yes, the crystal formations in sight now look like they did aeons ago . . . they are the same as when you were here before . . . this is the pathway to your own crystal palace. Walk more quickly now to the gate . . . swing it open with joy . . . the garden is the same as when you left it . . . the small pool of crystal water still sits by the emerald-clustered shrubs. Go over to the pool now . . . see how clear and pure it is . . . it shines like a mirror. Bend over and see yourself as you really are . . . yes, you see your true and perfect reflection now . . . your truly are home again. And listen . . . someone calls you . . .

there on the front porch stands your long-lost family . . . all smiling . . . waiting to greet you and love you . . . you run to them and enter into loving embraces for several minutes. Then you all enter your home . . . your beautiful crystal palace. It is even more magnificent inside . . . shimmering crystal walls . . . glittering crystal chandeliers . . . you walk through the familiar halls and rooms. As your tour is almost complete, you come to the room in the center of your home . . . the family chapel . . . complete with ancient tablets and symbolic stained-glass windows. Experience the chapel . . . kneel before the altar and offer the prayers of your family tradition up to the Most High Realms . . . feel the presence of Divine Love surround you. As you talk more with your family, share experiences with them before it is once again time to depart . . . knowing that you can return now any time you please. Wave farewell to them and your home as you close the gate . . . feel the happiness as you walk down the familiar pathway and out into the streets of the crystal city . . . experience a calm joy as you see the brilliant crystal city disappear into the heavens as you re-enter the crystal on your third eye. Feel a sense of true renewal as you enter your physical body once again . . . feel your breathing once again. You are back in the body now . . . but you will always be at home now, for you can return at any time . . . home to your crystal palace.

Awakening the Inner Crystal Meditation

The purpose of this meditation is to awaken the spiritual body by cleansing and purifying in the first step and by charging with White Light in the second step. The two crystals used to facilitate this process are to be clear, clean crystals that have been stored in salt for 24 hours prior to use. Put a crystal in each hand, holding it so that the thumb is resting comfortably on the largest facet of the crystal. Then get in a good, relaxing position for meditation; lying down works very well for this exercise of wholeness, but sitting may be used if desired.

Close the eyes and take a few deep breaths . . . inhale and exhale very slowly . . . letting the physical body flow in its natural rhythm. Begin concentrating on the crystal in the left hand . . . feel the

facet under the thumb . . . feel the energy. Feel the crystal beginning to resonate . . . feel it begin to draw the stress from your
being. Feel the body relaxing more and more . . . and as it relaxes,
feel the body resonating with the crystal . . . loosening all the
stress, negativity, tenseness, and dullness within the body. And as
these negative elements become loose and apart from the body to
which they were clinging . . . feel them gravitating towards the
crystal. Feel the toes and the feet . . . feel all negative elements
from the toes and the feet flowing out and into the legs. Then feel
all the negativity that has been stored for so long in the legs move
slowly up the legs and into the lower body. The lower body feels
heavy as the negativity gathers there . . . experience the heaviness . . . then experience how free it feels when the darkness and
negativity flows up the body to the chest area. Now focus your
attention to your right hand . . . feel the tips of your fingers and
your hands . . . feel the negativity, stress, and dullness being released and feel it all flowing up your right arm . . . as it flows,
your fingers, hands, and arms relax totally . . . becoming free and
clear of all negative elements. As the negativity moves out of the
arm and into the chest area, it joins with the other negativity
collected there . . . and it feels heavy, very heavy. Now the focus
is on the top of the head . . . the negative elements that have been
stored in your mind for so many, many years are now loose and
waiting to be drawn into the crystal in your left hand . . . slowly
the negative elements within your head move easily into the neck
and on into the chest. All the negative elements are now in the
chest and feeling heavy upon the body . . . but the heaviness soon
lifts as the negativity moves into the left arm . . . all the stress, the
tension, the darkness, the negativity of the entire body flows into
the crystal. Feel the coldness of the crystal in your left hand and
put it away from your body . . . and as you do, let your consciousness focus again on your being . . . feel the purity, the clarity, the
stillness. Spend a few moments bathing in this calm state of existence . . . and as you do, become aware of the pulsations of the
crystal in your right hand . . . feel the glittering crystalline energy
filling your right hand with energy and Light that you've never
before experienced. Feel every cell and every nerve in your right
hand vibrating with the crystal . . . sending out beams of pure

White Light up your right arm . . . it feels unlike anything you've ever felt before. And the vibrating White Light moves over the chest and into the left arm, down the arm, into the left hand and fingers . . . then flows swiftly back up the left arm and up into the neck and head. Open your eyes for a moment to see the sparkling white beams flying all around you . . . then close them to experience the full intensity of your new Light-mind. And the Light beams then flow quickly to the chest area and spin joyously over the heart center before moving down the entire body in waves of pure White Light . . . moving into the legs, feet, and toes . . . charging your entire body with Light . . . awakening completely your shining body of Light. Feel the energy whirling within you and all around you . . . feel yourself merging with the cosmos. You are no longer a part of the universe . . . you are the universe . . . you are a perfect crystal . . . you are Light and Love . . . you are . . . you are . . .

Stay in this ecstasy as long as you like . . . experience the crystal bliss totally. You are the Light . . . you are the Love . . . you are the universe. When you are ready, slowly become aware of your physical presence again . . . but in a new way . . . the Light-body will manifest itself on a physical level also. You are new . . . you are born again into a wonderful new body and life . . . feel it . . . experience the new you that is a part of the universe, that is the universe. Now feel the crystal in your right hand . . . it's warm and glowing . . . as are you. Put it aside . . . slowly open your eyes . . . arise . . . awaken to a new life . . .

After each meditation rinse both crystals in cold water and store them in salt for 24 hours . . . then use them again and again and again . . .

Cosmic Crystal Meditation

This meditation will enable you to experience the cosmos with the aid of your crystal . . . so, lay back, put your crystal, point up, at your crown chakra, relax, and prepare to have the adventure of your life . . . this is your chance to view in person what others write and read about. Just continue relaxing . . . close your eyes . . . breathe slowly. Feel the air around you . . . feel your connection with the universe. Breathe slowly and deeply . . . leaving the earthly realm behind . . . relaxing deeply . . . and more deeply . . . feeling your body beginning to blend with the air around you . . . blending and flowing more evenly now . . . breathing and being deeply a part of the universal flow. You feel the sense of true oneness now . . . a peace . . . a serenity. Now let your awareness drift slowly up into the crystal at your crown chakra . . . already it is flowing with a brilliant White Light and vibrating with cosmic energy from the higher realms. And as you enter the crystal . . . you, too, feel this White Light surround your entire being and you begin to vibrate gently with this newly found energy. Your entire being tingles as you feel the crystal begin to move . . . slowly at first . . . then gaining speed . . . until you look out of the windows of Light to find yourself racing through the atmosphere. The Earth is growing smaller and smaller . . . it looks like a shining blue and green marble . . . then a faint glimmer . . . then it disappears. Your attention is now focused on other planets . . . other moons. There is Venus . . . cool . . . blue . . . with a thin veil of shimmering silver woven around it. Now Mars is in sight . . . red and orange . . . a fiery and passionate planet. On you travel . . . Saturn is in front of you now . . . gaze at the whirling, multicolored rings . . . feel the energy being generated. Then prepare to leave this familiar galaxy as you soar to other realms . . . experience the quietness of space . . . even as meteors flash by you . . . leaving faint trails of cosmic Light . . . into the vastness . . . deeper and deeper into space. You're entering another galaxy now . . . you see bursts of bright colors . . . streams of Light . . . orbs of silver and gold . . . glowing spheres that emanate Light and Love. You see spaceships the size of Earth's moon moving quietly through the clear atmosphere . . . and smaller spacecrafts darting quickly about . . . sending beams of multicolored Light to you in your crystal. As you move through this galaxy you experience the ultra-high frequencies emitted by the beings here . . . it excites you and leaves you feeling at peace as you move on into space . . . moving more quickly now . . . Lights streaming by you. A kaleidoscope of images pass you . . . moving through brilliant galaxies quickly now . . . experiencing higher and higher octaves of Divine Love . . . moving quickly . . . quickly and swiftly . . . then breaking through the streams of Lights into a higher realm of Light-ness. A stillness . . . your crystal craft seems to have ceased moving . . . yet it moves . . . it moves in and with the energy of this intense Light . . . and you begin to move in the perfect rhythm of this Light. Experience the Light . . . the warmth . . . the highest Divine Love in the universe . . . flow with it for as long as you like. When you are ready to feel your own individual consciousness again . . . look out the windows of your crystal and see the Light moving again. As your crystal ship moves with the speed of Light now . . . you move through space and galaxy upon galaxy . . . you are Light . . . you are Divine Love . . . moving quickly and quietly into your own galaxy now . . . even the sun seems dull compared to your Light. You spiral around the sun three times and as you do . . . your crystal begins to travel more slowly now . . . spiraling slowly, seeing the beautiful green and blue orb of Earth clearly in sight now . . . spiraling into the misty atmosphere . . . and slowly, very slowly and gently the crystal is back in its place on your crown chakra. You once again enter your body . . . feeling the Light and energy and Divine Love of your journey still with you. Experience it throughout your body . . . let it flow from the crown chakra down into every other chakra of your body . . . filling you completely with the highest Love in the universe . . . now and forever . . .

Crystal Chakra Meditation

This meditation is based on the theory presented in Chapter 4 concerning the crystal chakras and can best be practice after reading that information.

Sit or lie in a comfortable position—sitting will probably work best for this meditation. Relax . . . breathe slowly and deeply . . . becoming more and more aware of your own being . . . of your chakras. Begin to feel them vibrate with energy . . . and feel that energy send out a bright White Light that surrounds your entire body . . . feel this Light while you relax more completely. Feel the Alpha Light energy in the crystal chakra below your sacral chakra . . . feel this intensity at the very core of your being. Then feel the energy vibrations in your sacral center . . . splenic center . . . solar plexus center . . . heart center . . . throat center . . . third-eye center . . . crown center . . . moving up to the Omega crystal chakra and feel the energy vibrating and sending radiant beams to the higher realms. Experience this awareness of your own chakra system for a few moments . . . relax in the Divine Love you now feel for yourself and the entire universe. Focus your attention once again on the gleaming crystal chakra above your crown center . . . feel it emanating and manifesting energy from the highest realms of the cosmos . . . it is alive with this brilliant white energy. Feel it completely as it begins to spiral down your entire being . . . spiraling around your crown center . . . on down to the third-eye center . . . to the throat now . . . down to the heart . . . spiraling around the solar plexus center . . . now the splenic center . . . down around the sacral chakra and spiraling gracefully into the base crystal chakra. When this powerful energy hits the core of your crystal chakra . . . an explosion of bright White Light occurs and the energy then shoots up the entire chakra system of your body with the speed of lightning. It shoots up through the crown center . . . up higher into the crystal chakra . . . up faster into the cosmos . . . blending into the power of the universe. You are blending with the cosmos . . . you are the universe now . . . you are complete . . . you are whole . . . you are . . . you are . . . you are . . . forever.

Healing Temple Journey

Close your eyes now . . . and begin to relax . . . starting to let go of tension, stress and distracting thoughts of the past or the future. Watch as the body and mind come into greater harmony . . . clarity . . . and union. Become more aware now of the subtle inner rhythms resonating throughout your entire being . . . relax into these rhythms . . . and allow each and every level of your being to blend and unite with one another . . . until you sense the reverberations of total harmony . . . and total peace. Sense your whole being as a symphony of bells resounding throughout a quiet meadow at dawn . . . enjoy these feelings of freedom and harmony. And now allow yourself to drift upwards . . . spiraling upward to unspeakably beautiful etheric realms . . . realms where clouds and rays of every color mix and blend their energies in a symphony of

Light . . . slowly unfolding into and through each other . . . grand mandalas of color flowing through one another . . . creating even more elegant and beautiful mandalas . . . patterns of perfection . . . ever-moving . . . ever-changing. A ray of bright White Light comes into your awareness now . . . pure White Light beckoning you to come forth . . . and as you come closer and closer . . . sense the powerful emanations calling to you . . . whispering of realms beyond. Becoming totally immersed in this shaft of White Light, you experience a sense of acceleration . . . exhilaration . . . as you pass through realm after celestial realm . . . all passing by so very quickly . . . knowing that your destination lies in even greater heights . . . in a great land of Light. Traveling at great speeds now . . . sensing the energies of your destination. And finally in a burst of Light . . . you enter this great celestial plane . . . a plane where every atom sparkles with the intensity of the ray of White Light that brought you here. It is as if hundreds of suns are shining their Light here all at one time . . . so powerful are these energies . . . the intensities of the Lights and the Sounds are almost too much to bear . . . until you let go of all resistance and allow it to flow through every atom of your being. Your awareness starts to perceive a great Healing Temple . . . calling you to come forth. Approaching it . . . a grand and glorious crystalline structure . . . receiving and projecting awesome rays of Light and Sound . . . it is as if this Healing Temple is the very nucleus of the energies of this entire celestial plane. A familiar tone reaches your awareness and calls you inside this vast structure . . . and finding yourself inside a healing chamber, one of many such chambers in this Healing Temple. Your own Higher Self has called you here to experience greater union with your Divine heritage . . . to experience a therapy that will help to activate and align your inherent spiritual abilities and talents . . . abilities and talents that will assist both you and your brothers and sisters on the Earth-plane to fulfill your spiritual quests for wholeness and union. Lie down now on the therapy table in the middle of the chamber . . . finding this table to be extremely comfortable and already humming with energy. The therapy begins as the light becomes subdued . . . your eyes close . . . and long, deep tones of sound start to fill the chamber . . . very soft at first . . . starting to blend with your own energies . . . and gradually building in intensity. Celestial tones and chords of sound and music flow through your whole being . . . becoming one with you . . . spiraling chords of music lift your spirit into even greater heights of awareness . . . every atom of your being is awake and alive as never before. As the music reaches a crescendo, streams of lightning-fast color rays are projected from above the therapy table. These multicolored rays shoot directly into each and every chakra simultaneously . . . filling them with rapid pulses of every color hue imaginable . . . these color pulses continue with rapid geometric precision . . . as the chakras start to glow more and more brightly with each passing moment. And now a special device above the therapy table projects three-dimensional mandalas of color and sound into each chakra by powerful laser beams . . . feel the mandalas enter into all seven chakras, transforming each one into geometrically-precise crystalline spheres of Light and Sound. Consciousness soars as you enter the Light-body of your own Higher Self . . . experiencing the power of Light and Love as you have never experienced it before . . . expanding now into a union and blending with the entire Healing Temple complex . . . feeling the awesome energies pulsing throughout the whole crystalline structure . . . experiencing the rays of cosmic Light and Sound being projected into the Healing Temple . . . reverberating throughout the entire complex . . . and emanating these rays outward to the many other Healing Temples that exist in other multidimensional planes and in other far-off galaxies. Feel the entire cosmic network of Healing Temples resounding throughout creation . . . each linked to one another . . . each united with all others throughout the Infinity of manifestation.

Notice, now, a thread of Light connected to your Earth-body . . . see this body as a true temple of Light . . . a Spirit-filled consciousness . . . connected to all the other temples throughout creation. Ride this ray of White Light now, going from the crystalline Healing Temple of the higher realms of Light . . . spiraling once again through the myriad levels and dimensions as you travel back to the Earth-plane . . . passing through whole dimensions in a second . . . whole galaxies in a flash . . . catching a brief glimpse of each. Continuing to follow the ray of Light connecting your own Higher Self to the Earth-body that is one aspect, one projection of your multidimension Higher Self . . . spiraling now into the physical body . . . becoming more aware of the sensation and movement of the breath passing slowly in and out of the body . . . feeling deeply relaxed . . . and retaining a sense of continuity and oneness with your own Higher Self. Gradually open your eyes . . . and see the Earth-plane with a new vision, a new perspective . . . knowing that the guidance and wisdom of your Higher Self is always there . . . always available . . . always your own true path towards wholeness.

NOTES

Foreword

1. Rupert Sheldrake, *A New Science of Life: The Hypothesis of Formative Causation* (Los Angeles: J.P. Tarcher, Inc., 1981), p. 186.
2. A. Holden and P. Sanger, *Crystals and Crystal Growing* (London: Heinemann, 1961), p. 80.

Preface

1. Beverly Criswell, *Quartz Crystals: A Celestial Point of View* (Reserve, N. Mex.: Lavandar Lines Corp., 1982), p. iv.

Chapter 1

1. Mircea Eliade, *Shamanism: Archaic Techniques of Ecstasy* (Princeton, N.J.: Bollingen Foundation, Princeton University Press, 1964), p. 4.
2. Joan Halifax, *Shamanic Voices* (New York: Dutton, 1979), p. 4.
3. Eliade, *Shamanism*, p. 137.
4. Ibid., p. 136.
5. Ibid., p. 138.
6. Ibid., p. 132.
7. Ibid., p. 47.
8. Michael Harner, *The Way of the Shaman* (New York: Bantam Books, 1980), p. 140.
9. Ibid., p. 140.
10. Ibid., p. 140.
11. Ibid., p. 139.
12. Eliade, *Shamanism* p. 339.
13. Harner, *Way of the Shaman*, p. 141.
14. Frank Dorland, "Rock Crystal: Nature's Holy Stone" (pamphlet), 1974, p. 2. Available from P.O. Box 6233, Los Osos, CA 93402.
15. Cornelius Hurlbut, *Minerals and Man* (New York: Random House, 1968), p. 228.
16. Mellie Uyldert, *The Magic of Precious Stones* (Wellingborough, Northamptonshire, England: Turnstone Press, 1981), p. 53.

17. Edgar Cayce, *Edgar Cayce on Atlantis* (New York: Warner Books, 1968), p. 89–90.
18. Ibid, p. 86.
19. Rev. Dr. Frank Alper, *Exploring Atlantis, Vol. 1* (Phoenix, Arizona: Arizona Metaphysical Society, 1982), Jan. 19, p. 4.
20. Ibid., August 24, p. 2.
21. Ibid., April 13, p. 1.
22. Ibid., Feb. 2, p. 3.
23. Joyce Petschek, *The Silver Bird: A Tale for Those Who Dream* (Millbrae, Calif.: Celestial Arts, 1981), p. 129.
24. Ernest L. Norman, "Amid the Pyramids," *New Atlantean Journal* 11, no. 4 (Winter 1983), p. 11.
25. Bill Cox, "Strange, Shadow-Like Pyramids Seen in Atlantic Crystal Ball," *Pyramid Guide*, no. 18; (Santa Barbara, Calif.: Life Understanding Foundation, 1975), p. 1.
26. Joan O'Connell, "The Crystal Skull," *New Atlantean Journal*, 11, no. 3 (Fall 1983), p. 14–15.
27. Brother Philip, *Secret of the Andes* (San Rafael, Calif.: Leaves of Grass Press, 1976), p. 20.
28. Cayce, *Cayce on Atlantis*, p. 90–91.
29. Joseph Whitfield, *The Treasure of El Dorado* (Washington, D.C.: Occidental Press, 1977), p. 181.
30. J. J. Hurtak, *The Book of Knowledge: The Keys of Enoch* (Los Gatos, Calif.: Academy for Future Science, 1977), p. 421.
31. Ibid., p. 421.
32. Ibid., p. 425.

Chapter 2

1. Hurtak, *The Book of Knowledge*, p. 22.
2. Dr. Serge de la Ferriere, *Psychological Works: No. 6—Universal Medicine: The Soul of Things* (Secaucus, N.J.: Lyle Stuart, Inc., 1969), p. 56.
3. Wally Richardson and Lenora Huett, *Spiritual Value of Gem Stones* (Marina del Rey, Calif.: DeVorss, 1980), p. 23.
4. Guy Murchie, *The Seven Mysteries of Life* (Boston: Houghton Mifflin, 1978), p. 449.
5. Halifax, *Shamanic Voices*, p. 14–15.
6. Virginia MacIvor and Sandra LaForest, *Vibrations: Healing Through Color, Homeopathy and Radionics* (New York: Samuel Weiser, 1977), p. 105.
7. Ibid., p. 104.
8. Ibid., p. 104.
9. Ibid., p. 105.
10. Benoytosh Bhattacharya, *Gem Therapy* (Calcutta: Firma KLM Private Limited, 1981), p. 8.
11. Roland Hunt, *The Seven Keys to Color Healing* (New York: Harper & Row, 1971), p. 113.
12. Criswell, *Quartz Crystals*, p. iv.

Chapter 3

1. Harner, *Way of the Shaman*, p. 144.
2. Murchie, *Seven Mysteries*, p. 453.
3. John White and Stanley Krippner, eds., *Future Science* (Garden City, N.Y.: Anchor Books, 1977), p. 216–217.
4. Murchie, *Seven Mysteries*, p. 453.
5. Albert Roy Davis and Walter Rawls, *Magnetism and Its Effects on the Living System* (Hicksville, N.Y.: Exposition Press, 1974), p. 124.
6. William Tiller, "A Lattice Model of Space," in *Phoenix: New Directions in the Study of Man* 2, no. 2 (Fall/Winter 1978), (Stanford, Calif.: Phoenix Associates), p. 28.
7. Glenn Clark, *The Man Who Tapped the Secrets of the Universe* (Marina del Rey, Calif.: DeVorss, 1955), p. 32.
8. Hurtak, *The Book of Knowledge*, p. 80.

Chapter 4

1. Ibid., p. 33.
2. Ibid., p. 105.
3. Ibid., p. 74.
4. Ibid., p. 74.
5. John Michell, *The View over Atlantis* (London, England: Abacus, 1975), p. 99.
6. Pat G. Flanagan, *Beyond Pyramid Power* (Marina del Rey, Calif.: DeVorss, 1975), p. 37.
7. Michell, *View over Atlantis*, p. 105.
8. Mark 4:30–32, Oxford Annotated Bible.
9. Ibid., p. 99.
10. Sananda, from personal communication to authors, December 3, 1982.
11. Hurtak, *The Book of Knowledge*, p. 73.
12. Dee Jay Nelson and David Coville, *Life Force in the Great Pyramids* (Marina del Rey, Calif.: DeVorss, 1977), p. 111.
13. Hurtak, *The Book of Knowledge*, p. 40.
14. Ibid., p. 33.
15. Ibid., p. 232.
16. Ibid., p. 173.

Chapter 5

1. *Gems, Stones and Metals* (Virginia Beach, Va.: Heritage Publications, 1977), p. 7–8.
2. Alper, *Exploring Atlantis, Vol. 1*, Jan. 26, p. 3–4.
3. Petschek, *Silver Bird*, p. 129.
4. Bill Kaunitz, "Rock Crystal," *Crystal Keys, 1* (February 1981), p. 3.
5. Roland Hunt, *Fragrant and Radiant Healing Symphony* (Sussex, England: Academy of the Science of Man, 1949), p. 38.
6. Highly recommended are Bill Schul and Ed Pettit, *Pyramids and the Second Reality* (New York: Fawcett Columbine Books, 1979) and Dee Jay Nelson and David Coville, *Life Force in the Great Pyramids* (Marina del Rey, Calif.: DeVorss, 1977).

7. Petschek, *Silver Bird*, p. 125.
8. Rev. Dr. Frank Alper, *Exploring Atlantis, Vol. 2* (Phoenix, Ariz.: Arizona Metaphysical Society, 1983), p. 70.
9. Owen Davies ed. *The Omni Book of Computers and Robots* (New York, N.Y.: Zebra Books, Kensington Publishing, 1981), p. 43.
10. Alper, *Exploring Atlantis, Vol. 1*, Feb. 16, p. 4.
11. Ibid.
12. Uyldert, *Magic of Precious Stones*, p. 68.
13. Albert Roy Davis and Walter Rawls *The Rainbow in Your Hands* (Hicksville, N.Y.: Exposition Press, 1976), chap. 3.
14. Criswell, *Quartz Crystals*, p. 3.
15. Davis and Rawls, *Rainbow in Your Hands*, pp. 48–49.
16. Carol and Warren Klausner, "Marcel Vogel III—Crystal Workshop" (cassette tape of February 1983 workshop, San Diego, Calif.).
17. Alper, *Exploring Atlantis, Vol. 2*, p. 16.
18. Brother Philip, *Secret of the Andes*, pp. 13–14.
19. Alper, *Exploring Atlantis, Vol. 2*, pp. 22–23.
20. Richard Bach, *Illusions* (New York: Delacorte Press, 1977), p. 97.
21. Ibid., p. 134.
22. Ibid., pp. 86–87.
23. Ibid., p. 92.
24. Bhattacharya, *Gem Therapy*, p. 9.
25. Bill Cox, "Crystals, Form and Psychic Energy," *Pyramid Guide 16* (Santa Barbara, Calif.: 1975), p. 4.
26. Davis and Rawls, *Rainbow in Your Hands*, p. 50.
27. Hurlbut, *Minerals and Man*, p. 239.
28. John Sinkankas, *Minerology for Amateurs* (Princeton, N.J.: Van Nostrand, 1964), p. 437.
29. Ibid., p. 437.
30. Hurlbut, *Minerals and Man*, p. 240.
31. Ibid., pp. 239–240.
32. Alper, *Exploring Atlantis, Vol. 1*, March 2, p. 3.
33. *Gems, Stones and Metals*, pp. 30–31.

Chapter 6

1. Murchie, *Seven Mysteries*, p. 641.
2. Uyldert, *Magic of Precious Stones*, p. 52.
3. Moira Timms, *Prophecies and Predictions: Everyone's Guide to the Coming World Changes* (Santa Cruz, Calif.: Unity Press, 1980), p. 123.
4. Louis Acker, "Paraphysics and New Energy Technologies" (pamphlet), 1980, p. 23. Available from P.O. Box 81, Chichester, NY 12416.
5. Hurtak, *The Book of Knowledge*, p. 547.
6. Baron Karl von Reichenback, *The Mysterious Odic Force* (New York: Samuel Weiser, 1955), p. 23.
7. Richardson and Huett, *Spiritual Value of Gem Stones*, p. 135.
8. Thea Alexander, *2150 A.D.* (New York: Warner Books, 1976), p. 105.
9. Acker, "Paraphysics," p. 43.
10. Don Robbins, "Quartz Influencing Earth Currents," *Pyramid Guide 39* (Santa Barbara, Calif.: 1979), p. 8.

11. Petschek, *Silver Birds*, p. 145.
12. Barbara Burke, "The Mightiest Memory Yet," *Science Digest*, December 1983, pp. 44–45.
13. Hurtak, *The Book of Knowledge*, p. 489.
14. Tuella, *Project: World Evacuation* (Deming, New Mex.: Guardian Action Publishers, 1982), pp. 40–41.
15. Bill Cox, "The Wonderous Rife Microscope," *Pyramid Guide 22* (Santa Barbara, Calif.: 1976), p. 2.
16. Karl Schutte and John Myers, *Metabolic Aspects of Health* (Kentfield, Calif.: Discovery Press, 1979), p. 245.
17. Acker, "Paraphysics," p. 64.
18. Murchie, *Seven Mysteries*, p. 639.
19. Klausner, Vogel tapes.
20. Bill Cox, "Today's Thoughtography, Tomorrow's Thought-Viewer," *Pyramid Guide 24* (Santa Barbara, Calif.: 1976), p. 1.
21. Murchie, *Seven Mysteries*, p. 453.
22. "High-Power Fiber Aids Laser Processing," *High Technology*, November 1983, p. 13.
23. Dan Winter, "To Be Crystal Clear," (Eden, N.Y.: 1981), p. 14.
24. *Gems, Stones, and Metals*, p. 32.
25. Joan O'Connell, "Crystal Power!" *New Atlantean Journal* 11, no. 2 (Summer 1983), p. 9.
26. Ancient Mysteries Research Institute, "The Ancient Temples as Living Entities," *New Atlantean Journal* 11, no. 4 (Winter 1983), p. 37.
27. Hurtak, *The Book of Knowledge*, p. 321.
28. Hunt, *Fragrant and Radiant Healing Symphony*, p. 105.
29. Richard Wolkomir, "Amazing Superstuff," *Omni*, November 1983, p. 180.
30. Acker, p. 60.
31. Ruth Montgomery, *Threshold to Tomorrow* (New York: G.P. Putnam's Sons, 1982), p. 130.
32. Alper, *Exploring Atlantis Vol. 1*, Jan. 26, p. 1.
33. Hurtak, *The Book of Knowledge*, p. 80.
34. Ronald Brown, *Lasers: Tools of Modern Technology* (Garden City, N.Y.: Doubleday, 1968), p. 179.
35. Petschek, *Silver Bird*, p. 147.
36. Acker, p. 44.
37. Alexander, *2150 A.D.*, p. 77.

GLOSSARY

alchemy: the science of transformation and transmutation, especially involving the infusion of greater degrees of Light into matter and consciousness.

Alpha: the beginning of a cycle of evolution.

auric system: the totality of energetic functions within human consciousness. Includes the physical body as one of the multitudinous levels of vibrational patternings.

biosatellite: a Light-body of multidimensional projection capabilities.

capacitor: a nonconducting substance that can store energy as a result of oppositely charged conducting substances that are on either side of the nonconductor.

consciousness cell: the primary unit of consciousness. The energetic counterpart of the biological cell, it is a whole unto itself and also acts in synergetic harmony with the million myriads of consciousness cells composing all creation.

cosmology: a belief system concerning the metaphysical-spiritual nature of reality.

dodecahedron: a geometric solid having twelve plane faces.

Divine Intelligence: synonymous with Universal Mind. The all-encompassing crystalline matrix of Intelligence pervading every atom of creation.

esoteric vs. exoteric: the inner, metaphysical nature of manifestation versus the physical, exterior characteristics.

Eye of Yahweh: the central point of Divine Intelligence within every aspect of every level of creation.

fourth dimension: a term used to denote the next quantum octave of existence from the three-dimensional Earth-plane.

frequency: the number of repetitions of a periodic process in a unit of time, such as cycles per second.

gemology: the science of gems.

harmonics: integral multiples of an original frequency.

Higher Self: that aspect of each individual that is in direct contact with the highest levels of Divine Intelligence—the "Master" within every person.

holography: the generation of holistic images with vibrational interference patterns.

homeostasis: a dynamic state of equilibrium.

human bio-energetic system: synonymous with the human auric system. The synergic union of the biochemical and energetic levels of human functioning.

initiation: the quantum re-organization of crystalline order to a higher, more encompassing level of Divine Intelligence.

interference pattern: the multiplanar patterns formed by intersecting vibrational frequencies.

lapidary: a cutter, polisher, or engraver of precious stones.

laser: *l*ight *a*mplification by *s*timulated *e*mission of *r*adiation. A device that generates and projects highly coherent, ordered frequencies of Light.

Light-body: the body that consciousness inhabits on the fourth-dimensional levels.

living Light: Light infused with life-giving, life-sustaining and life-evolving properties.

metallurgy: the science and technology of metals.

modulate: to regulate or modify energy.

multiplex: to transmit several distinct messages on the same channel or circuit simultaneously.

Omega: the end of an evolutionary cycle, leading into the beginning of another cycle.

piezoelectric effect: an electrical charge created by mechanical deformation or the mechanical stress caused by an electrical charge.

Pyramid of Light: the basic functional unit, or base harmonic, of all intelligence functions of the Universal Mind.

pyramidology: the science of pyramidal energy dynamics.

refraction: the bend or deflection of an energy wave as it enters a medium of different density, e.g., from air into water.

superholographic: the multiplexing of multiple holograms on one or more dimensional planes.

synergy: the cooperative action of multiple agents such that the total effect is greater than the sum of the individual parts.

transduction: the conversion of one form of energy into another, e.g., Light frequencies into mechanical vibrations.

unified energy field: a field of wholeness that resonates with the unity inherent within every aspect of manifestation.

Universal Mind: see Divine Intelligence.

vortex: a time-space-gravity gradient area in which an interdimensional "doorway" is created. These are centers of programming and communication.

Whole-Light Synthesis: the holistic synergetic unity of manifestation.

BIBLIOGRAPHY

Acker, Louis. "Paraphysics and New Energy Technologies." Chichester, New York, 1980.

Alexander, Thea. *2150 A.D.* New York: Warner Books, 1976.

Alper, Rev. Dr. Frank. *Exploring Atlantis, Vol. 1*, Phoenix, Arizona: Arizona Metaphysical Society, 1982.

Alper, Rev. Dr. Frank. *Exploring Atlantis, Vol. 2*, Phoenix, Arizona: Arizona Metaphysical Society, 1983.

Bach, Richard. *Illusions*. New York: Delacorte Press, 1977.

Ballard, Juliet Brooke. *The Hidden Laws of Earth*. Virginia Beach, Va.: A.R.E. Press, 1979.

Ballentine, Rudolph. *Science of Breath*. Honesdale, Pa.: Himalayan International Institute of Yoga Science and Philosophy, 1977.

Bentov, Itzhak. *Stalking the Wild Pendulum*. New York: Dutton, 1977.

Bentov, Itzhak. *A Cosmic Book: On the Mechanics of Creation*. New York: Dutton, 1982.

Bhattacharya, Benoytosh. *Teletherapy*. Calcutta: Firma KLM Private Limited, 1977.

Bhattacharya, Benoytosh. *Gem Therapy*. Calcutta: Firma KLM Private Limited, 1981.

Brother Phillip. *Secret of the Andes*. San Rafael, Calif.: Leaves of Grass Press, 1976.

Brown, Ronald. *Lasers: Tools of Modern Technology*. Garden City, N.Y.: Doubleday, 1968.

Brown, Ronald. *Telecommunications: The Booming Technology*. Garden City, N.Y.: Doubleday, 1970.

Bryant, Page. *Crystals and Their Use: A Study of At-One-Ment with the Mineral Kingdom*. Sedona, Ariz.: Network for Co-operative Education, 1982.

Burr, Dr. Harold Saxton. *The Fields of Life*. New York: Ballantine Books, 1973.

Cairns-Smith, Alexander. *The Life Puzzle*. Edinburgh, Scotland: Oliver and Boyd, 1971.

Capra, Fritjof. *The Tao of Physics*. Boulder, Colo.: Shambala Publications, 1975.

Cayce, Edgar. *Edgar Cayce on Atlantis.* New York: Warner Books, 1968.

Cox, Bill, ed. *Pyramid Guide* Vols. 1–9. Santa Barbara, Calif.: Life Understanding Foundation, 1974–1979.

Criswell, Beverly. *Quartz Crystals: A Celestial Point of View.* Reserve, N. Mex.: Lavandar Lines Corp., 1982.

Critchlow, Keith. *Time Stands Still: New Light on Megalithic Science.* New York: St. Martin's Press, 1982.

Davidson, D., and H. Aldersmith. *The Great Pyramid: Its Divine Message.* London: Williams and Norgate, 1936.

Davies, Owen, ed. *The Omni Book of Computers and Robots.* New York: Zebra Books, Kensington Publishing, 1981.

Davis, Albert Roy, and Walter Rawls. *Magnetism and Its Effects on the Living System.* Hicksville, N.Y.: Exposition Press, 1974.

Davis, Albert Roy, and Walter Rawls. *The Rainbow in Your Hands.* Hicksville, N.Y.: Exposition Press, 1976.

Eliade, Mircea. *Shamanism: Archaic Techniques of Ecstasy.* Princeton, N.J.: Bollingen Foundation, Princeton University Press, 1964.

Ferguson, Marilyn. *The Aquarian Conspiracy: Personal and Social Transformation in the 1980s.* Los Angeles: J. P. Tarcher, Inc., 1980.

Ferriere, Dr. Serge de la. *Psychological Works: No. 6—Universal Medicine: The Soul of Things.* Secaucus, N.J.: Lyle Stuart, Inc., 1969.

Flanagan, Pat G. *Pyramid Power.* Marina del Rey, Calif.: DeVorss, 1975.

Garvin, Richard. *The Crystal Skull.* New York: Pocket Books, 1973.

Gems and Stones. Virginia Beach, Va.: A.R.E. Press, 1979.

Gems, Stones and Metals. Virginia Beach, Va.: Heritage Publications, 1977.

Glick, Joel. *Healing Stoned.* Albuquerque, N. Mex.: Brotherhood of Life, 1981.

Halifax, Joan. *Shamanic Voices.* New York: Dutton, 1979.

Hall, Manley P. *The Inner Lives of Minerals, Plants and Animals.* Los Angeles: Philosophical Research Society, 1973.

Halpern, Steven. *Tuning the Human Instrument.* Belmont, Calif.: Spectrum Research Institute, 1978.

Harner, Michael. *The Way of the Shaman.* New York: Bantam Books, 1980.

Heline, Corinne. *Music: The Keynote of Human Evolution.* La Canada, Calif.: New Age Press, 1976.

Hills, Christopher. *Secrets of the Life Force.* Boulder Creek, Calif.: University of the Trees Press, 1979.

Holden, A., and P. Sanger. *Crystals and Crystal Growing.* London: Heinemann, 1961.

Horn, Delton. *Basic Electronics Theory.* Blue Ridge Summit, Pa.: TAB Books, 1981.

Hunt, Inez, and Wanetta Draper. *Lightning in His Hand: The Life Story of Nikola Tesla.* Hawthorne, Calif.: Omni Publications, 1964.

Hunt, Roland. *Fragrant and Radiant Healing Symphony.* Sussex, England: Academy of the Science of Man, 1949.

Hunt, Roland. *The Seven Keys to Color Healing.* New York: Harper & Row, 1971.

Hurlbut, Cornelius. *Minerals and Man*. New York: Random House, 1968.

Hurtak, J. J. *The Book of Knowledge: The Keys of Enoch*. Los Gatos, Calif.: Academy for Future Science, 1977.

Isaacs, Thelma. *Gemstones, Crystals and Healing*. Black Mountain, N.C.: Lorien House, 1982.

Jenkins, Francis, and Harvey White. *Fundamentals of Optics*. New York: McGraw-Hill, 1976.

Kaunitz, Bill. *Crystal Keys*, Vol. 1. February 1983.

Krieger, Dolores. *The Therapeutic Touch*. Englewood Cliffs, N.J.: Prentice-Hall, 1979.

Krippner, Stanley, and Daniel Rubin, eds. *The Kirlian Aura*. Garden City, N.Y.: Anchor Books, 1974.

Larsen, Stephen. *The Shaman's Doorway*. New York: Harper & Row, 1976.

MacIvor, Virginia, and Sandra La Forest. *Vibrations: Healing Through Color, Homeopathy and Radionics*. New York: Samuel Weiser, 1977.

Michell, John. *The View over Atlantis*. London, England: Abacus, 1975.

Montgomery, Ruth. *Threshold to Tomorrow*. New York: G. P. Putnam's Sons, 1982.

Murchie, Guy. *The Seven Mysteries of Life*. Boston: Houghton Mifflin, 1978.

Nelson, Dee Jay, and David Coville. *Life Force in the Great Pyramids*. Marina del Rey, Calif.: DeVorss, 1977.

O'Donoghue, Michael. *The Encyclopedia of Minerals and Gemstones*. New York: Putnam, 1976.

Ott, John. *Health and Light*. New York: Pocket Books, 1973.

Ott, John. *Light, Radiation and You*. Old Greenwich, Conn.: Devin-Adair, 1982.

Pennick, Nigel. *Sacred Geometry*. San Francisco: Harper & Row, 1980.

Petschek, Joyce. *The Silver Bird: A Tale for Those Who Dream*. Millbrae, Calif.: Celestial Arts, 1981.

Richardson, Wally, and Lenora Huett. *Spiritual Value of Gem Stones*. Marina del Rey, Calif.: DeVorss, 1980.

Saunders, Albert. *Working With Semiconductors*. Blue Ridge Summit, Pa.: TAB Books, 1969.

Shul, Bill, and Ed Pettit. *The Secret Power of Pyramids*. Greenwich, Conn.: Fawcett Publications, 1975.

Schutte, Karl, and John Myers. *Metabolic Aspects of Health*. Kentfield, Calif.: Discovery Press, 1979.

Sheldrake, Rupert. *A New Science of Life: The Hypothesis of Formative Causation*. Los Angeles: J. P. Tarcher, Inc., 1981.

Sinkankas, John. *Mineralogy for Amateurs*. Princeton, N.J.: Van Nostrand, 1964.

Sorrell, Charles. *Rocks and Minerals*. New York: Golden Press, 1973.

Spalding, Baird T. *Life and Teachings of the Masters of the Far East*. Marina del Rey, Calif.: DeVorss, 1964.

Spangler, David. *Explorations: Emerging Aspects of the New Culture*. The Park, Forres, Scotland: Findhorn Publications, 1980.

Talbot, Michael. *Mysticism and the New Physics*. New York: Bantam Books, 1981.

Timms, Moira. *Prophecies and Predictions: Everyone's Guide to the Coming World Changes*. Santa Cruz, Calif.: Unity Press, 1980.

Tisserand, Robert. *The Art of Aromatherapy*. New York: Inner Traditions International, 1979.

Tompkins, Peter, and Christopher Bird. *The Secret Life of Plants*. New York: Avon Books, 1973.

Tuella. *Project: World Evacuation*. Deming, N. Mex.: Guardian Action Publishers, 1982.

Uyldert, Mellie. *The Magic of Precious Stones*. Wellingborough, Northamptonshire, England: Turnstone Press, 1981.

von Reichenback, Baron Karl. *The Mysterious Odic Force*. New York: Samuel Weiser, 1955.

Weil, Robert, ed. *The Omni Future Almanac*. New York: World Almanac Publications, 1982.

White, John, and Stanley Krippner, eds. *Future Science*. Garden City, N.Y.: Anchor Books, 1977.

Whitfield, Joseph. *The Treasure of El Dorado*. Washington, D.C.: Occidental Press, 1977.

Williams, Gilbert. *Celestial Visitations*. Corte Madera, Calif.: Pomegranate Books, 1979.

Winter, Dan. "To Be Crystal Clear." Eden, New York, 1981.

About the Authors

Dr. Randall N. Baer (Mechail) is both a naturopathic doctor and a spiritual scientist concerned with developing new avenues for the integration of the worlds of high-technology science, spiritual wisdom, and holistic healing modalities. A widely traveled student and teacher, he has participated in the programs of numerous learning centers in the United States and England, gaining degrees and certifications in a broad range of disciplines. Among others, these include a B.A. degree in Religious Studies from Carleton College in Northfield, Minnesota, and an N.D. degree from Brantridge Forest School in Sussex, England. Now based in northern New Mexico, he continues research and development of innovative Light-based therapies and inventions. One therapy currently in use is "Light Transformational Therapy," which is designed for spiritual activation and alignment. It integrates the elements of chromatics, lumia, pyramidology, crystal energetics, radionics, sonics and aromatherapy into a unified "healing temple chamber." This therapy has proven to be quite successful in catalyzing the balanced unfoldment of spiritual growth in an accelerated manner. Other related therapies are in various stages of research, development and utilization, incorporating such fields as computers, lasers, holography, fiber optics, flotation tanks, accelerated learning and healing techniques, and consciousness research. Also, in addition to presenting workshops and lectures on crystals, healing temple therapies, and Divine Science, he is codirector of the Temple of Divine Science, a project dedicated to scientific and consciousness transformations based upon applied spiritual knowledge integrated with today's high-technology.

Vicki Vittitow Baer (Andronica) has been a channel for various aspects of the Spiritual Hierarchy of Light for over a decade. During this time she has been deeply involved with the rebirth of knowledge concerning the multifaceted levels of Divine Science and healintemple therapies. As codirector of the Temple of Divine Science, she is actively working to bring the Light-based technologies of ancient history and the celestial realms back to the Earth-plane as an integral element toward catalyzing a new era of consciousness transformation.

For more information regarding workshops, lectures, consultations, or the Temple of Divine Science, write to:

Dr. Randall and Vicki Baer
P. O. Box 1339
Los Alamos, New Mexico 87544

The Crystal Connection Newsletter

A newsletter called the *Crystal Connection* is made available at periodic intervals by the authors. It includes information on experimental results, new ideas and inventions, resource references, channelings, and updates on the activities of the authors. There is no subscription, the only requisite being the sending of a self-addressed, stamped envelope (legal size) for each issue. To receive the next issue, write:

Crystal Connection Newsletter
P. O. Box 1339
Los Alamos, New Mexico 87544